M000095426

CHURCH AFTER

CHURCH AFTER

*Finding transformation in
unexpected change*

ANNA MITCHELL HALL

Cane Mill Press

Copyright © 2021 by Anna Hall

All rights reserved. No part of this book may be reproduced in any manner whatsoever without written permission except in the case of brief quotations embodied in critical articles and reviews.

First Printing, 2021

Cane Mill Press
Scottdale, GA 30079
www.canemillpress.com
editor@canemillpress.com

Library of Congress Control Number: 2021914829

ISBN/SKU 978-1-7375604-0-1
EISBN 978-1-7375604-1-8

CONTENTS

With thanks to Jim, my parents, Oakhurst Baptist Church, Cameron Trimble and our team at Convergence, the 3rd Thursday Book Club, my adventure partner Laura, and everyone else who has helped me along the way.

PREFACE

Everything old has passed away; see, everything has become new.
-2 Corinthians 5:17-19, New Revised Standard Version[1]

We are living in a time when change seems to be waiting for us around every corner.

In 2020, the world came to a halt due to a global pandemic. School buildings shuttered, and learning moved online. Work went remote for many, and, for those working in essential roles, the threat of illness made every single day stranger and more stressful than the one before. Most of us stopped socializing with those outside our home, going months without seeing our beloved family and friends. Our favorite traditions, from dining out to sports to church, were interrupted and reinterpreted. We attended worship in our homes while simultaneously singing God's song in the strange lands of Zoom and YouTube. By our microphones and cameras, we sat down and wept with joy at weddings, baptisms, and ordinations, and with sorrow at funerals and the final services of dying congregations. This change was at a speed and on a scale that humanity and the church had not seen in at least a few generations.

As I write this, my family and I have been vaccinated against the virus. While I am celebrating, I am still grieving all that we have lost and unclear about what the future will hold. I am clear, however, that our future will contain further unexpected changes for me and for my faith community.

We humans have a mixed and complicated relationship with change. In the United States, we careen from electing leaders promising change to electing those dedicated to reversing those changes. We want the change we want, but only if those things that comfort us can remain the same.

Despite our complicated personal and political attitudes, change is inevitable. No president, or anyone else, has enough power to prevent change. Every generation since the industrial revolution has lived lives that were greatly changed from the lives of their parents and grandparents. Technological change has seemed to accelerate the process even faster in the twentieth century, to the point that each micro-generation is notable for what technology has been a part of their lives since birth. Yet, the skills needed for surviving and thriving during change are the same ones that allowed every one of our ancestors to live into their new generation.

What does this have to do with the modern Christian church?

Everything.

If a congregation is alive, in the sense that it still meets in some way to practice the Christian faith together, it will face frequent and often unexpected change. Change is a fundamental element of Christianity, a faith that has been claimed by generation upon generation that came before us. Some Christian voices might say that Christianity only speaks against change and worships a God and set of rules that can never change. Yet more and more Christian voices are realizing that God still speaks and speaks in new ways.

I am reminded of a poem by Jalaluddin Rumi, a Sufi poet who lived almost 1000 years ago, in this beloved translation by Coleman Barks.

This being human is a guest house.
Every morning a new arrival.
A joy, a depression, a meanness,
some momentary awareness comes
as an unexpected visitor.
Welcome and entertain them all!

Even if they're a crowd of sorrows,
who violently sweep your house
empty of its furniture,
still, treat each guest honorably.
He may be clearing you out
for some new delight.
The dark thought, the shame, the malice,
meet them at the door laughing,
and invite them in.
Be grateful for whoever comes,
because each has been sent
as a guide from beyond.[2]

While we cannot control when and how change will come to visit, if we are willing to welcome such an unexpected visitor, we may hear in its voice a new awareness, guiding us in our next steps, and yes, even helping us learn to embrace change.

| 1 |

Introduction

Unexpected change occurs daily in churches. Highly publicized examples of congregational change make headlines, from pastors who find themselves mired in sexual scandals to congregations who must relinquish their shining cathedrals because of financial instability. These examples may seem particularly dramatic, yet any time a congregation encounters a big change, this encounter can be a profound experience for those deeply involved. While initial reactions may be negative, especially for those of us who prefer to know what to expect at every turn, these changes can be more than trials to get through. Each unexpected change in a congregation can be a chance to learn more about how to follow the God that makes all things new.

Like the disciples, who struggled to adapt after Jesus' death and resurrection, with the added challenge of struggling to understand much of the wisdom He had left with them, every day, churches are charged with continuing in the face of losing a leader, a building, a group of congregants who leave the church. This book is for your church, so you can learn together from the change you are facing now and changes you will face in your future. This book is for churches who seek to prepare their people to listen to and learn from God during all the changes life will throw at them.

The following chapters can be used in the order they are presented or taken one at a time if a particular topic is of more interest to you. There are reflection questions throughout and at the end of each chapter for those who choose to use this book as a workbook. In the Appendix, there is a small group curriculum for those who would like to do a group study of this material. Also in the Appendix are a change assessment for your congregation, worship resources, and a brief curriculum for use with children and youth during times of congregational change.

In **The Challenge of Change,** I discuss why change is so hard and yet so important for us as individuals and churches. I outline the latest research on how our brains process change and suggest some ways we can draw on the Christian story to help us recognize change as the gift that it can be.

In **The Power of Change,** I explore the power of using transitions intentionally to develop change-ready Christians. I suggest structures to move beyond survival into intentional transformation during congregational change. These structures focus on building skills for change and adaptation. There is great potential for individual and congregational transformation in unexpected congregational change. Strategic approaches to learning during transition can encourage individual and congregational transformation. Becoming intentional about learning and transformation during transition can equip congregants to better handle change whenever it comes.

In **Facing Change,** I provide recommendations on how to deal with a current change in ways that can cultivate transformation. When you allow time and energy for learning about your congregation, tuning up congregational systems, and planning rituals and celebrations, you make room for big things to happen in your members' hearts and minds.

In **Embracing Change,** I provide recommendations for enhancing learning in members during congregational change. This section addresses how members learn through various elements of worship and spiritual practice and provides practical suggestions for developing these areas in your congregation.

In **Practicing Change**, I address the need to build in practices of support and guidance for your members to access during times of change. Whether the change they are facing is congregational or individual, such as an illness, job loss, or relationship shift, you can ensure that they are supported and guided through that change by church leaders and fellow members. Learning from change often starts in encounters with others or with spirit. Providing opportunities for those encounters is an essential part of faith formation.

In **Helping Children and Youth with Change**, I examine the possibility of using congregational change as an opportunity for learning among children and youth in the congregation. Strategies and best practices for religious education and youth programming are included.

In **Cultivating Change Readiness,** I describe how you can build change skills in your congregation even when you are not facing a big change. Change-ready congregations are sustainable congregations, and while it may seem like quite a large endeavor, you will not regret shifting time and energy to this effort. The next time a big change comes around, your congregation will approach it with open minds, open hearts, and maybe even enthusiasm!

Throughout, I return to stories of the members of Smalltown Baptist Church, Suburban Presbyterian Church, and Urban Congregational Church. While these stories are specific and grounded in their individual contexts, they contain universal themes and experiences that will illustrate the conclusions and recommendations that follow.

I wrote this book out of my deep concern for the future of congregations. Organizations, including churches, that cannot change and adapt will die. Christians who cannot change and learn will be unable to carry the faith into the future. If any form of church is to survive into the future, Christians who can handle change and harness it for real learning and transformation will be the key to that survival.

It is my hope that this book contains resources for the work of envisioning, building, and strengthening congregations that create just those Christians. Such Christians, ready to face change and transition with open minds and tools for learning, will lay the foundation for Christianity to survive and thrive in the coming years, decades, and beyond. Above all, I hope the experiences of the churches I studied and the resources provided here will help you and your congregation to face change with hope, optimism, and even excitement about the amazing opportunity ahead for you and all in your congregation to become the change-ready Christians that our faith needs for the future.

| 2 |

The Challenge of Change

Everyone deals with change differently, and some are more comfortable with change than others. Often the way change transforms us (or doesn't) depends on whether we see it as a good or bad thing.

Personally, I hate change. When I hear about something that is changing, that is out of my control – something at work, my bus route, a technology I use, or a tool I rely on – I get very weird. I start to feel all hot and flushed. I immediately get aggravated with whoever caused this change or even the person delivering the news of the change. I begin thinking of who I can blame and where I can lodge an official complaint. I generally come to acceptance at some point, but my initial reaction is 100% fight or flight. Certainly, as a researcher of pastoral transitions and someone who really enjoys observing and participating in organizational change, I obviously do not hate all change. Yet when you get down to the nitty-gritty of changes that affect my life and are not in my control in any way whatsoever, I am not a big fan.

In my years of studying and working on change, though, I found out a few essentials about change that shifted my perspective. I began to understand from my research and experiences that:

- Change can and should be an integral part of any faith journey.
- Change can be a living devotional.

5

- Change can be the raw material that is transformed into new insights and awareness.
- Change can bring us closer to our fellow Jesus followers, from the beginning of our faith until today.

When we find ways to see and live through a change in these ways, it can be a powerful tool for our personal and congregational development.

So how can we shift our perspective on change?

Change and our Christian Story

Change is built into the story we live as Christians. The disciples experienced change on the road to Emmaus. They were working to process what they believed had happened to Jesus, having heard things that were beyond their comprehension and possibly beyond their belief. They could not incorporate this new information, the words of the women and their vision telling them Jesus was alive, their checking the tomb and finding it empty, into what they believed had happened, that Jesus had been killed by the authorities and would be with them no more on this journey they had chosen because of his call. Even when they met who they believed to be a stranger on the road, they could not process that this stranger was, in fact, Jesus. Assuming him a true stranger, they told him the whole story. The story of the trauma of their beloved rabbi being put to death, the story of their hopes and dreams for him, the story of their ongoing confusion. Jesus had some more lessons for them. He told them that not believing the women, or their own eyes was foolish and slow of heart. That not taking this new information and incorporating it with what they knew of the scriptures was the wrong path. But despite all these disorienting experiences, it was not until Jesus broke bread with them, as he had so many times before, did they find a new understanding that while Jesus was killed, he had not left them. He was walking with them into their future.

How many times are we faced with change, with new information, only to compare it with what we already know and either discard new conflicting data or simply doubt that data's truthfulness or relevance? We are just like Jesus' disciples every single day. We doubt that God is in the change until we have a transforming experience or insight that opens our eyes. The only problem is that too often, we don't have those mountaintop experiences. We go along unchanged, even resisting change, and never learning how God may be speaking to us in the process.

Big Changes Ahead

One of the primary changes we face as members or leaders of churches is a change in pastors. Like the disciples, who struggled with change after Jesus' death and resurrection, with the added challenge of struggling to understand much of the wisdom He had left with them, churches are charged with continuing after the loss of one teacher to continue to spread the good news of their faith through the life of the church. During such transitions, some people find their faith tried or strengthened by their experiences during the transition. But even when their experiences have the potential for profound learning, people consistently interpret their experiences considering their pre-existing beliefs.

Struggling with any information that conflicted with those beliefs, seeking out research and information to shore up their pre-existing beliefs, they put all new information in a box marked "Don't need, don't want," high up on a shelf somewhere. In churches, this can seem benevolent. People want to see a congregation in the best light, so they ignore information that might counter that. But it can hinder their progress. People who want to think of themselves as generous cannot figure out why their salary is not enough to attract the best candidates. Lay leaders who think of themselves as reasonable and forward-thinking seek a pastor who will continue business as usual.

Changing our Minds

The disciples could not take in the new information of the women's testimony, the empty tomb, the appearance of Jesus. Not at first. They had new information, sure, but they took it, compared it to what they believed to be true, and dismissed any parts that did not fit. We all do that. Brain research has suggested that not only do humans amplify information that confirms their beliefs, we experience genuine pleasure – the same brain chemical released from pleasure or a substance high – when processing information that supports their beliefs.[3]

During the run-up to the 2004 presidential election, Emory researchers found just that. While undergoing an fMRI brain scan, 30 men with strong political feelings had to evaluate statements by both George W. Bush and John Kerry in which the candidates clearly contradicted themselves. The Republicans were critical of Kerry, the Democratic subjects were critical of Bush, yet both neatly avoided criticizing "their guy." And the scans of their brain showed the part of the brain most associated with reasoning was inactive during all of this. Most active were the parts responsible for emotions, conflict resolution, and making judgments about morality. Once the men had arrived at a conclusion that made them emotionally comfortable, their reward and pleasure centers lit right up.[4]

We all do this. In some ways, we are just rats in a maze of life, avoiding the shock of information that conflicts with our beliefs to get to the pleasure of reaffirming what we already believe to be true. This is the challenge we have with our experiences of change. We go in with one idea of what is or should be unfolding and have an exceedingly difficult time opening ourselves to any new information from the change that, while it may be shocking or unexpected, can be one of our greatest sources of learning. Yet we are called by the stories of our faith to transcend our instincts to take the safer path and avoid the shock. In fact, our faith is permeated with the idea of *metanoia*, an idea that closely parallels what we would now call transformational learning.

Learning from Experience

For many people, learning from change, if it happens at all, is not transformative. Our frames of belief and understanding persist in the face of informal and incidental learning, despite experiences and new knowledge that challenge those frames. In my study of several congregations experiencing a pastoral transition, congregation members seemed to interpret most of their learning during the transition through the lens of their pre-existing frame of reference, if the lesson even intersected with their frame at all.

Research on transformative learning shows that most learning is transactional rather than transformative. Transactional learning is where learning through experience only results in new skills or information.[5] In my study, for example, congregation members reported a great deal of learning that simply obtained information or skills needed to move forward in their responsibilities to the congregation. Even disorienting experiences such as learning of the changes in gay marriage policy in the national church or feeling much less comfortable in the congregation during the transition were likely to be interpreted through the lens of their frame of reference and reinforce that frame, rather than change it significantly.

In the field of neuroscience, brain imaging research has demonstrated that strongly-held beliefs are not only difficult to change, but that brain processes actively resist changing them. Parts of the brain that handle reasoning are less active when we are faced with information that challenges our strongly-held positions. We experience an emotional shock, almost as if we are a rat in a science experiment choosing the wrong path in the maze. The most active areas as we take in this challenging information are those dedicated to handling emotions and resolving conflict, followed by activity in the pleasure area when the conflict is believed to be resolved.[6] We love this feeling of rejecting the new information or making it match what we already believe. Echoing this brain research on issues about which my study members felt the most strongly, such as their beliefs about God and their belief in the rightness of gay marriage, no changes in frames of reference were seen. In fact, a member of one church did seem to enjoy their efforts investigating national church policy and deeming it unconstitutional, thus supporting the rightness of their positions against gay marriage. More on that later.

Finding the transformation in change

My experiences in churches during transitions changed me and the path of my life in significant ways. In the first congregation where I experienced a pastoral transition as a member, the challenges shaped my understanding of how congregations cope with unexpected change. Before that, vandalism and the congregation's and community's response formed my beliefs on resilience and cooperation across differences. My experiences working at a church in transition grew my understanding of how congregations work and make decisions together on small and large issues every day. Was I transformed by each of these experiences? I took from them a firm belief in the power of a small group of people working together for good. I also witnessed how hateful acts, and even internal conflict, can bring a community together to stand for love.

According to scholar Barbara J. Fleischer, the entire biblical narrative of Jesus' encounters with the disciples describes a teacher preparing his students for a profoundly changed way of life. He challenged his listeners to see a new reality of graciousness, transform their perspectives, and live according to this broader vision of life. Fleischer compares this way of changing the disciples" minds to the theory of transformative learning, which says that learning which transforms our beliefs and actions must be disorienting.[7] There is no way to get to the transformation without the disorientation. And Jesus' life and words continually provoked disorientation in his followers, challenging their small views of God and how others were lacking in the eyes of God.

The beautiful thing about the transformative lessons of Jesus is that they not only changed the disciples but confronted the small-minded and oppressive authorities and power structures of the time. These teachings led to Jesus' death at the hands of those authorities. Then we find ourselves back again on the road to Emmaus, as disciples who are finally disoriented enough to see through their shock toward the lessons of following Jesus on a post-resurrection journey. They were able to change their minds. And so can we.

In the following chapters, you will hear how three quite different congregations navigated the unexpected change of a pastoral transition. How they learned or did not learn from their experiences. And whether they were transformed. These congregational experiences will serve as our companions throughout the book, as we explore how to not only navigate unexpected changes successfully but how to use them as an opportunity for congregational transformation, as a chance to follow Jesus on a new road.

Let's get traveling.

Reflection Questions:

- How do you feel when things in your life change?
- Are you thrown for a loop?
- Or do you love that feeling of navigating new territory?

| 3 |

Smalltown First Baptist Church: "seeing God's will manifested"

Smalltown First Baptist Church sits a block off the main street in a small foothills town of a southern state. The campus, made up of two red brick buildings and a connecting wing, sits at a busy red-light intersection and faces a Walgreens across the street. Its next-door neighbor is a CVS. The leftmost building is clearly the newer, with a contemporary but traditional church appearance, faced with a columned porch and topped with a tall white steeple. The building to its right has the appearance of being the original sanctuary, having a mock columned entrance with an arched window above a double French door.

On entering the church, a spacious two-story atrium filled with light from the multiple French entry doors and windows above contains a round table with information about the church, a few formal sofas, and a few older gentlemen welcoming and passing out bulletins. Opposite the entry doors isare a set of French doors and just past them, two sets of stairs, all three providing entry into the sanctuary. Upon entering the sanctuary, the space opens up, with high ceilings rising to a center point, three sections of pew seating, and a front raised area containing a podium, choir loft, and several chairs. This area is backed by a baptismal font centered behind the altar, with a piano off to the left and an organ to the right. The space has a golden glow from yellow paint and amber woodwork.

A typical service is full, with an almost exclusively white congregation of 150-200 in attendance, and begins with music, often trumpet. Much of the service is liturgical. At one point, all the children are invited to come down for a children's sermon, which is amplified for the whole congregation to hear. The children then leave while the adults hear a sermon. Communion, offered only on occasional Sundays, is passed around in small cups with wafers, and the celebrant blesses them once all are handed out, at which point the congregants eat and drink them. Hymns are traditional and tend toward those written in the late 19th and early 20th centuries. There are no screens or other multimedia components to the sanctuary or the service.

Smalltown through the Eyes of Members

Valerie, a young woman in her 20s, is a teacher in the local schools. Valerie described the church as, "a second home. . . . I think a lot of people would too, because all of the programs that they have and everything that we have, and we offer to people. . . . I feel very comfortable here. I get excited to come here. . . . It's not a Southern Baptist church, but it's not really new age either, kind of somewhere in the middle. I always say we still use a hymnal . . . we still have a hymnal. We don't have worship and praise music that often."

Ted, who served for years as music minister of the church and served on the search committee for the next pastor, said the church is "a mainline Baptist church the way Baptist churches used to be and this one still is. . . . Worship style is still traditional, which is much less common than it used to be. . . . We don't even have a projection system in the sanctuary. It wasn't done as a symbol. We didn't need it, so we didn't put one in. We did spend two hundred thousand dollars on a pipe organ, which is also sort of indicative of where we are worship style. . . . We have people that . . . drive down here because they want that kind of worship and they also want to be in a moderate church. They want to be Baptist."

A Change in Pastors at Smalltown: A Season of Transitions

In May 2013, on Mother's Day, the pastor of Smalltown announced from the pulpit that he would be retiring at the end of June. Members described learning that the pastor was going to leave. Jack, a younger retiree and active lay leader who took on additional roles during the transition, remembered the announcement on Sunday morning that the pastor was leaving. "Our pastor totally out of the blue [for] most of us, but I think it's all of us, . . . walked in on Mother's Day morning and said that he was resigning effective the end of June. That caught our entire congregation by surprise. We had all these other positions that were already vacant or occupied by interims. . . . That caught us very much off guard, so there was a lot of shock and awe I guess in the congregation." Valerie observed, "I guess it was more abruptly . . . in our eyes. When you don't know what goes on behind the scenes and someone just comes in on Sunday and he's like, 'You know, it's my time to go.' He had been here for a while, but it just seemed like, "Oh my goodness." You couldn't believe that was happening. . . . It's hard when they do come in on Sunday and it's like, 'Okay, after the last final song of this Sunday, we have to go into church conference.' You just get this feeling like, 'Oh, it's happening.'"

This was a season of multiple transitions for Smalltown. Between 2013 and 2015, every staff position turned over at least once. Smalltown's long-time music minister had retired during 2013, and the church was already searching for a children's minister when the pastor announced his retirement. Both positions were filled during 2014. By early 2014, the youth minister and administrative assistant positions were vacant as well, and the children's minister hired the previous year departed the church in September. Christine, a long-time member a little over 90 years old, remembers, "The most recent transition really started with the children and youth minister. . . . They did not form a committee at first to replace her . . . Then about three months after she resigned, the music minister that had been here thirty-seven years . . . retired. . . . That was a big transition, but we had an excellent interim music minister, and he was with us for just over a year, and then the pastor resigned. . . . Since then, we've been really in an upheaval because of the changes that were just taking place."

Getting the work done

Jack described trying to figure out how to get the work of the church done without a pastor. He said first, they worked on "identifying where the holes were." He said their next step was "getting people to step up and fill the holes, and they did." Christine elaborated that "we had to have a lot of volunteers doing things that we didn't have a trained professional to do . . . because it takes that . . . On two cases where they just volunteered and told the congregation, if you would like, I will do this. One was the Wednesday night Bible Study Service, because in the process of losing the staff members, we had [lost] . . . prominent members that filled a lot of these jobs. This one young man stepped up and said that he would do the Wednesday night Bible Study for us, and he was excellent. He filled in for all those months until the pastor came. The other one . . . This man stepped up and he knew how to do it, and he was our volunteer administrator until the pastor came. . . . [T]hey felt led to do it and the church was delighted to have them do it." She was sometimes surprised by who stepped up to help, "we had some people step up that we wouldn't have thought would fill in like that, really good people."

Smalltown's lay leaders then had to determine the next steps for securing a new pastor. In June, the congregation held its first informational session on the search for a new pastor and took nominations for a committee to search for an interim pastor. By September, the church had formed a search committee and by October, located an interim pastor. The interim pastor at Smalltown was not full-time but was responsible for most of the preaching and some visiting duties during his tenure.

A member of the search committee described how the committee acquired the information they needed on the congregation's preferences for the new pastor. "We prepared and distributed a survey throughout the congregation, . . . we listed characteristics of a pastor and asked them to write those characteristics, what is the most important characteristic . . . I think there were eight or nine things on the list. Then we compiled the results. Some of the folks on our committee were really good at that kind of thing, so we compiled the results." They used the information acquired from this survey to shape their next steps to narrow down their list of candidates. "We asked our top ten candidates to also fill out that survey and to rate themselves without telling them how the congregation had voted, of course, and to also elaborate on that. Why what you list as number one, number two, number three. Why do you list that way? Why is this characteristic important to you? It was very, some of them lined up so beautifully . . . Some didn't at all."

Member experiences

Christine recalled learning about the progress of the search process through hearing from the search committee during announcements at worship and events. She said the search committee "just told us a month or so before after they got all the resumes in and all the computer things, Internet things. They just told us that they had eliminated it down to five and they were considering those five and that they were looking to eliminate it to one or two." She went on, "they eliminated it to one really quick and they were really shocked and pleased when they had the vote."

Valerie learned about the process by observing her husband's work on the search committee. Valerie remembered, "It did seem like it was very involved. My husband met all the time. I mean, they had meetings almost every Sunday. If they didn't have meetings on Sunday, they would be doing something at home. It just seemed like that they were continually busy, but it was a long process." She reported a lesson drawn from her observations intersecting with her personal experiences as a teacher, "I didn't realize that there were that many potential candidates. I've come from the teacher perspective and there are's tons of people who are willing to be a teacher but . . . the number of resumes and seeing the amount of people and then different people that I know. You know that people are coming to visit and they're preaching because they want to be here type of thing. You know they're trying to impress you. It was just interesting seeing the amount of people that were interested. It's a good thing because people want to be a part of your church or want to come here." She pointed to a larger lesson learned, "if you're wanting to find the right person, I know you've got to take the steps it takes to get there." She went into further detail later in the interview, saying, "Before, I didn't understand much about the whole process at all. I just knew this person was leaving and this person would come in. Now, I just think I know more about the process in general. I understand when a new preacher comes, different things will happen. I guess the whole process is different for me because before, I just pass it on, 'We'll find somebody else.' Now, you actually are more genuinely invested in who you're having in the church. Not that it didn't mean more then, but it means more now to you because in my situation, I think, if I were to have a family, that type of thing, you think through all these things, 'Is this the right step?'"

Christine also recalled special meetings designed to inform the congregation. "Sometimes there was a special forum called. We've had what we call forums on Sunday morning about once a quarter, and we would have congregation meal and then discuss business. It was not a business meeting. It was just a forum and so we learned a lot that way." She went on, "And then they often came on Wednesday nights in between the Sundays to tell us things to keep us up to date. That was done by either committee chairman or somebody on the committee and the deacons." She remembered, "We could also ask questions if we needed to on Wednesday nights. We didn't do that much on Sunday morning, but we could at least know." She said after every announcement, they "always said you can come to the members of this committee and ask questions, or you can come to the deacons and ask questions or both, whatever you need to do. They were open to questions and opinions."

Christine particularly learned from these communications about the role of the congregational survey in the search process and about the congregation based on the results of the survey. She explained, "They used those surveys to determine how the committee would look for a pastor and that was input from the congregation itself and they said it was very helpful to have that survey that they did." She described the data collection process of the search committee, remembering that the committee "handed it out on Sunday mornings and it was on the Internet, on the e-mail, that thing. Everybody had access to it, and they gave us a couple of weeks or so to look it over and turn it in. It was picked up on a Sunday morning and then the committee put it all together and went over the thing." Christine said she learned from this survey report that "the congregation wanted a shepherd. I guess, the second most had something to do with his preaching. . . . it was interesting that it came out that the congregation really was anxious to have a real pastor shepherd."

In another conversation with one of the search committee, she recalled hearing "They were surprised about some of the priorities, how the priorities stacked up, because I had one of them say that it was surprising it ended up the way it did." She interpreted that information to mean "that they didn't know the congregation as well as they thought they did until they did the survey and we'd never had anything like this."

A new pastor for Smalltown

This committee worked together for 7 months and then, in May 2014, announced that they had identified a candidate for the new pastor. In early June, the congregation was given information about the candidate and invited to participate in a Q and A session with the deacons about the candidate and the process. In late June, the candidate came to town for a *candidating* weekend, which included meeting with various leadership bodies and a reception to introduce him to the congregation, along with preaching in the worship service that Sunday morning. The reception for the candidate was of the drop-in variety, with light snacks and sweets provided. The candidate stood in a receiving line of sorts as people stopped in to introduce themselves and ask questions. After that worship service, the congregation could vote on whether to call the candidate and voted in favor of his call. There was an enthusiastic round of applause after the vote, and all were invited to speak to the new pastor and his family in a receiving line after the service. The new pastor began his tenure in late July.

| 4 |

The Power of Change

As you can see from the story of Smalltown Baptist, in times of transition church members are learning. The challenge is that without any support or facilitation, they are learning things that may be inaccurate, unhelpful, and lack spiritual meaning. It is up to church leaders to create structures to help members learn in ways that increase understanding, deepen congregational engagement, and enhance their faith.

Learning from experience is an essential part of the Christian faith journey. Certainly, we all have stories of experiences that awakened us to a new way of thinking. Some of those experiences are big, like spending a night wrestling with fear in hopes of grabbing a blessing for the days to come, or an appointment spent receiving a good or bad diagnosis. Others are small, like a new coworker, a change in neighborhood, or simply growing older. Our reactions to these experiences can vary. We don't learn in healthy ways every time we experience change.

As Christians, we are called to new lives every day, and the rhythms of our years are shaped by a story of death and new life. So, grabbing hold of the transformation possible in the changes that come into our lives can be a crucial part of our faith formation. Jesus calls us to be willing to be disoriented, and to then to re-evaluate our current beliefs. To repent and change our minds. And learning, at its heart, literally changes our minds.

Yet all too often, we get stuck.

We never reevaluate the things we think we know. We fail to take in new information in a way that allows us to change our minds. Sometimes we simply stop, stuck in our tracks, refusing to change when change comes, railing at the winds.

Other times, we may learn and even be transformed by even the smallest changes in our lives. A friend of mine, David, who works as a business consultant, had his eyes opened to a community of homeless men living in a park after he simply changed the way he drove to work. He formed relationships with them and eventually, in partnership with the congregation where he was a member, founded and directed an organization called The River, dedicated to helping people without homes through relationship building with those who are housed. This organization has worked with other local groups to help their friends who live outside access both services and a community of caring friends to improve their quality of life. In some cases, this means they move off the street into housing. In other cases, they remain outside for now but benefit greatly from their new community in terms of jobs or benefits needed to live as well as possible for their situation. More recently, David helped found a community center in a neighborhood where people are at a high risk of displacement and homelessness, to work on the systemic issues underlying precarious housing situations. A simple alteration of his route to work has now impacted many of David's friends, both those who live outside and those who share his vision for relationship across boundaries. We never really know when change will bring an opportunity for amazing things.

Learning during transitions

In the three churches I studied, I found that members definitely learned during the transition. They primarily learned about their congregation and about the mechanics of pastoral transitions. They also learned about different preaching styles, about their church's larger denomination, and occasionally, about their faith.

It is exciting that even without support, members were learning about their congregation and their faith. However, the things they learned were occasionally incorrect and sometimes even problematic. Depending on the content of that learning, these lessons could be detrimental to the well-being of those members and the congregation as a whole.

One of the challenges of member learning during transitions is how much of it occurs through individual and, only occasionally, mutual work to make meaning out of unexpected events. Without support from scriptural or theological ideas, this meaning-making at best reinforces existing beliefs and at worst leads to a more negative impression of the congregation and its leaders. Those in my study who experienced deeper levels of meaning-making typically did so without any church leader involvement or support.

Barriers to learning from change

It is obvious that we do not always learn, even in very disorienting situations. Our human brains have some natural resistance to change.

Recent neuroscience research can explain some of our resistance to change. Our brains try extremely hard to protect us from danger. One way our brains do that is to flag anything that conflicts with our existing understandings as an error. This is done by activating our emotional brain activity in the amygdala and decreasing our rational brain activity in the prefrontal cortex. New information is harder to process and can exhaust our memory and processing. Our brains also pay more attention to negative input than positive. This is important in learning to avoid touching hot stoves, but counterproductive in other areas of our lives, particularly in our need to press through discomfort of change to learn what it has to teach us. [8]

In an example of these brain processes at work, one member of Suburban Presbyterian sought out a great deal of information on the changing policies regarding same-sex marriage within his church's larger denomination, the Presbyterian Church USA. Yet no matter how much time he spent investigating, he reported that he could not find any information on the arguments for legalizing same-sex marriage within that church structure. The information on these other positions was out there; a cursory internet search on my part found them quickly, but his frame of reference regarding what was acceptable Christian practice did not allow him to acknowledge them at all. His approach to gathering information, in fact, served to simply reinforce his existing frame of reference that there could be no logical justification for the opposing position. **To be clear, evaluating evidence and not changing one's mind on a big issue is completely ok. Being blind to even discovering the arguments of the opposing position prevents one from a greater understanding of the world in which we live.**

Without some intervention, big changes will not always lead to learning that is healthy and beneficial for the congregation and its members. It is only when we support that learning that those of us with leadership responsibilities in the congregation can ensure that change in our church leads to transformative learning in our members.

Supports and structures that help church members learn from change

Three key approaches can help your church members learn in ways that support their faith during or after big changes:

1. Take time to process.

People are most likely to learn from change when they take time to process the experience. On a personal level, this means:

- Feeling the ending.
- Refusing to rush the middle.
- Planning for the new beginning.

As William Bridges highlights in his groundbreaking works on life transitions, when we do not appreciate the need to fully experience and process every aspect of a life change or transition, we are likely to rush through it and be discouraged if we can't do so. We may feel confused, disoriented, and want to rush through or abandon the situation. But we lose much opportunity when we try to rush transitions. Particularly when we do not take time to leverage the in-between times. Bridges describes this in-between time as a neutral zone, and explains, "Painful though it often is, the neutral zone is the individuals and the organization's best chance for creativity, renewal, and development."[9]

Jesus went into the desert for 40 days and fasted and prayed before beginning his public ministry. *He honored the need to process this change in direction, before embarking on a new way of being in the world.*

In churches, taking this time to process has often taken the form of a lengthy interim ministry after a pastor's departure that allows for time to grieve and process together what this means for the congregation, communally and as individuals. However, in the face of the knowledge that every year of interim ministry can mean up to a 25% decline in member engagement and giving, that method of taking time is not as practical for modern churches.[10]

Also, during many big changes, the pastor is not the change! Our recent experiences with doing church in different ways due to a pandemic are a change in methods, not staffing. Other examples include a changing neighborhood, an offer from a developer to buy the property, or a fire or natural disaster. In these cases, walking through change will be done with the same leadership from before the change.

Yet time can still be taken to process the experience of transition if the congregation is intentional about it. Being intentional about time to process transitions means having a game plan long before a big change takes place. In the life of any church, opportunities to process the experience should become a regular part of the life of the community. At Smalltown Baptist, Christine explained how talking to other members helped build a sense of love and reassurance during the transition. "You always have close friends and they're the ones you talked to . . . that's who your friends are. I guess we had to reassure each other, and there's more people doing the reassuring than there were people that were really uptight about it."

While some people will take the time and have the connections to process the experience of change informally in their existing groups, for others, intentional structures for talking through their experiences will be needed. Such opportunities might look like the small group curriculum included with this book, weekly prayer, and listening sessions before or after worship or during the week, or an invitation for a facilitator or consultant to hold regular sessions with the congregation. This may be as short as 8-12 weeks, but trust me, the shortness of time is no excuse not to take it on. Remember, Jesus only had 40 days to have some profound spiritual experiences, and your congregation can do the same in the time you have.

2. Tell your stories – to yourself and others.

Telling the story of our experiences of change can also help with learning and transformation. Studies have shown that writing about or talking about such experiences, particularly when using storytelling or metaphor, helped people make meaning out of their transitions.[11]

We hear in Genesis about Jacob and Esau, about a time when a man, Jacob, feared his brother Esau so much that he was willing to sacrifice half his flocks and family as human shields, sending them out before him just in case his brother was feeling vengeful and murderous. Jacob, though, had an encounter on the road as he waited his turn to meet his brother, an encounter that changed him profoundly. He wrestled with a being that he called an angel all night. This experience marked his body and changed his name. How do we know of this transformation? He named the place it happened Penuel, which means "I have seen God face to face, and my life is preserved." In this way, his story was told through future generations whenever anyone asked the origin of the name.

We hear in Luke about a leper, healed by Jesus, as were so many. But this encounter changes more than his health. He is filled with gratitude and we know this because he walks back to tell his story and give thanks to the man who changed his life.

In my own research, Gail from Urban Congregational told of lessons learned from a time when people shared stories during worship.

> *"I think I learned how important it is for us to share our personal stories as far as like our spiritual journey......... That kind of let me see that everyone is so different even though it may not be diverse in age or race, culture, background or whatever, it's very different and where everyone comes from, like their perspective, but at the same time it's relatable."*

Simply talking about change experiences in a group can help surface the emotions and impressions that change brings. Again, a congregation need not pause for a year or more to incorporate storytelling into its transition experience. Simply offer opportunities to tell the stories of your lives together. Offer other opportunities to tell the stories of feelings and other things left unsaid, to and among each other. Offer the opportunity to tell the stories of the church collectively. All of this can be accomplished in only a few sessions over a few months but can have an enormous impact on the possibility of learning from change. If those in your congregation are worried that such storytelling will lead to gripe sessions or unhealthy conflict, a trained outside facilitator can help make these sessions healthy and constructive, rather than destructive, to your congregation and the relationships within it.

3. Practice reflection

Transformative learning requires critical reflection. We learn best when we reflect on how change intersects our ideas, beliefs, and frames of reference. We can critically examine the new ideas our experience is forming in us and avoid simply shoring up what we already believe. We can keep an eye out for points at which your new experiences might be showing us a new way of thinking. We can stay open to changing our beliefs and ideas. We can take notes, so we can fully process all these reflections, or talk about them with others.

We know a few things from research about how to do this sort of critical reflection in groups. Transformative learning in groups typically results from high-stakes events and working on meaningful problems together.[12] A big transition is certainly an occasion that can become meaningful collective work for the congregation, if it is structured and facilitated in that direction. Even with a congregation fully engaged in the work of transition, critical reflection, or going deep together into how each person's experiences intersect with their frames of reference, is crucial. Also key is member support for one another as they make meaning out of experiences of change and how they are learning from them.[13]

At Smalltown Baptist Church, Ted, who led their search committee, remembered that after the vote to select the new pastor,

> "Through this, especially there toward the end, we talked a lot about clarity and discerning God's will. We said . . .this trite thing that every pastor search committee everywhere says. "We know God's already picked this person out. We've just got to find the person." It is trite but it is also very true. We knew that God wasn't going to gift wrap this and say, 'Here he is.' Although, it was almost that way." He went on to describe the search process, saying, "It was one of the clearest times of my life of seeing God's will manifested. There have been some other times in other situations down through the years, but that was a very clear time." He went on, "I consider that part of the God work. Where God helps make things happen. I don't think God ever forces anything, but I think that goes against his nature, the way he chooses to deal with us, but he certainly put those pieces in place."

It is possible that Ted could have drawn these conclusions on his own, but conversation with other committee members about the role of God and the role of their work in the future of the congregation framed the eventual outcome as "God work" for him.

This type of collective reflection is not easy work, and it takes creating a culture of collaboration, trust, and honesty to even attempt it. In a loving community like a congregation, can we feel safe enough when thinking "you know, I thought that, but I am realizing I was wrong" to say those words out loud? Can we feel held enough to stay in the discomfort of change long enough to pass through it to the other side? Getting to that point will take intentional effort on the part of congregational leaders: first to build that culture, and then to guide the reflection needed. Professional facilitators can also be helpful in this process.

The good news about learning from change

A big change in the life of our congregation can leave us shocked, confused, and feeling lost, just like the disciples after the crucifixion of Jesus. The fantastic news is that learning together during experiences of change and transition can help members of any organization develop change skills they can use going forward. They will become better equipped to handle transition and change and learn from those experiences whenever they encounter them.[14]

Doing the work of facilitating learning from change is worth it, not only for the particular transition you may be facing this year, but for all life's changes facing your congregation and its members in the years to come. With the knowledge of Jesus' call toward transformation, an understanding of the need to continually repent or change our minds, and a loving community for support, our congregations can find new understanding on the other side of whatever unexpected change comes our way.

Reflection Questions

- Are some changes acceptable to you where others are frustrating, exhausting, or anxiety-producing?
- What differentiates "good change" from "bad change" for you?

| 5 |

Facing Change

So . . .your church is facing a big change right now. It may be expected or may have taken your congregation completely by surprise. It may be shared with many other congregations, like the return to buildings and programming after the Covid-19 pandemic, or the ongoing decline in congregational membership and attendance in the United States. It may be externally generated, like a natural disaster or changing neighborhood, or it may be internal, such as a change in pastors or a church split. It may be unique to your congregation and your denomination, geographical or cultural context.

Whatever change you are facing, it will benefit your congregation immensely if you can become intentional about how you move through this period of change. Intentionality during times of change can not only make for a smoother transition to what lies beyond, but also lead to transformation for the congregation and its members. Individual members and the congregation as a whole can learn, grow, and change in positive ways. A church can find renewed vitality and sense of mission.

When members learn from change, the congregation benefits. Learning can propel members toward greater spiritual development if their churches are able to support them appropriately. Learning can also strengthen congregational health, building toward a more unified mission and healthy dynamics.

Transitions can be a prime opportunity for churches to learn about themselves as organizations. According to Mead, pastoral transition in particular can be "a rich time for a congregation to update its perception of itself. It is a time to learn what new kinds of people have become part of their life . . . what has happened to the profile of ages in the congregation and the kinds of work the people are engaged in, . . . [to get] a new fix on what is going on in the community in which this local church is geographically located."[15] Other kinds of change can similarly provide opportunities for this type of discernment and focus, if we are willing to engage in the work.

This is fantastic news for you and your congregation as you face this change!

But it also means you have work to do.

Unfortunately, most congregations lack intentional support for growth and learning during times of transition. To support learning and transformation during big congregational changes, congregations must intentionally:

- Acknowledge and celebrate what has gone before.
- Work to increase member knowledge of the congregation and its context.
- Create opportunities for collective discernment around the future.
- Celebrate the new thing that is happening.
- Build healthy processes for organizational change. (Adapted from Mead)

In the pages ahead I will break down each of these further, but I hope you see a pattern here. Resisting or pretending that the change is not occurring will only hinder your congregation's growth and vitality. If you take the time to think through each of these elements, though, you will find a stronger congregation on the other side of the change.

Acknowledge and celebrate what has gone before

No matter how young or old your congregation is, you have a history that is worth celebrating. How did your congregation get started? What are the most meaningful moments that occurred between then and now? Remembering the history of the church can begin to build a consciousness of resilience rather than fragility and fear. Even if yours is a fairly recent church plant, there were moments along the way where you made big decisions, faced challenges, and journeyed through change. Make a list of those moments and think about how you might speak those stories into this present season of change. Could you create articles for your newsletter, record short videos of people telling their stories of the past, or build storytelling into your worship services? Celebrate your triumphs and your challenges, as it takes both to form a congregation over its history. Every congregation's journeys, and the milestones along the way, are worth celebrating.

Pay attention to recent challenges. Rather than pretending everything was hunky-dory until this current change, surface and honor declines, conflicts, and departures that may be still echoing through the life of your congregation. Without attention to the full reality of the congregation's recent context, any new changes will not be fully processed in healthy ways. When we have unspoken truths, or "elephants in the room," our whole selves are not incorporated into the process of change, limiting transformation and often deepening division or disconnection among members.

Who have been your "saints?" This may not be the language your congregation uses, but every church has those who have been stalwart supporters and workers over the life of the congregation. Whether you do this routinely or not, times of change are the perfect occasion for celebrating these folks. In my own congregation, we have used awards called "Heart of Oakhurst" awards to reward those who have gotten us where we are today. With a luncheon, recognition, and sometimes physical items to award, we make it clear how thankful we are for those who serve the church faithfully and often remarkably. One year, during which we transitioned our structure and bylaws to a new streamlined system, we decided to award everyone who had served in leadership that year, in honor of their faithfulness and dedication in such a time of change. We had a shared meal, a time of acknowledgement where each name was read and the recipient stood for a round of applause, and we gave each "Heart of Oakhurst" a gift certificate for Just Bakery, a program launched by our church to teach refugees baking skills and pay them fair wages. This gave the church a moment away from the work to rejoice and celebrate each other and the good things that come out of our work together.

Whether you are celebrating a retirement, the ending of a beloved church program or the leaving of a building, have cake and recognize all that you have gained through ministry together. Sing a few songs and/or tell stories together of your shared history. You will find that people will remember the celebrations long after the hard struggles have faded in their memory, and celebrations will become a part of the church's story going forward.

Work to increase member knowledge of the congregation and its context

During times of change, it is also important to remember the old saying, "Know thyself." A congregation often struggles with change when it does not face the change standing strongly in its own story and identity. I recommend using surveys, small groups, and/or interview projects to help your congregation get to know itself and its context.

Churches who are searching for a new pastor often undertake a survey to discern their needs and preferences, so that the search committee can use that information to identify the best candidates for the new pastor. I think going beyond this surface level, to truly understand the characteristics of the church and its members, is important for any type of transition. In my work with Convergence, I have developed a Vital Church Assessment that uses survey and other methodology to help a congregation understand its vitality in many areas: membership and attendance, engagement in church activities, engagement with external community, neighborhood context, finances, facilities, conflict history and skills, change skills, level of welcome, and member perceptions of the church's future. There are other assessments on the market as well. I recommend a comprehensive church assessment to any congregation facing significant change. We cannot respond authentically and in healthy ways if we do not have a healthy understanding of who we are.

For congregations who prefer self-study, there are other options. In small groups, members and friends of the congregation can do their own research and discernment around some of the areas mentioned above. As they participate in prayer walking the church's neighborhood, sharing testimonies to celebrate what has come before, and discerning what programs of the church are essential for a vital future, among other activities, participants will gain an understanding of the congregation and where it stands in relation to the change ahead. My organization, Convergence, provides such a framework in our reVision program, which I helped develop.

An additional option is a church and community interview project. I first learned of such projects from Rev. Stacy Harwell-Dye, who oversaw church and community interviews as part of a Roving Listener Project at Centenary United Methodist Church in Macon, Georgia. This church was situated in a neighborhood that had changed around it over the years, becoming under-resourced and disconnected from the church. To address this situation, the church began conducting interviews, first among members, then with members of the surrounding community, and then community members were recruited as interviewers so that the information gathering could reach deep into the community. Interviews asked about passions and dreams for the neighborhood, skills, and assets that interviewees had to offer, and willingness to share those in collective work together. Interviews were not used for evangelism but to build up the community, foster belonging and pride in the neighborhood, and help local residents have a voice. The church found itself and the neighborhood strengthened and transformed through this process.[16]

Once your congregation has explored its history and identity, it can explore together how members are experiencing a time of change. The Church After Curriculum for Small Groups, provided in the Appendix, offers one framework for this process. Building in times of storytelling, reflection, ritual, and mutual support, participants can find out more about each other, discover the gifts of transitions, and provide mutual support for the challenges and struggles of change.

However your church chooses to get to know itself and its context, the most important thing is that you do not skip this stage of your journey through change. We can only face the new when we have a clear idea of who we are, how we got here, and what we have to offer.

Create opportunities for collective discernment around the future

From the Quaker tradition of Clearness Committees to practice groups such as Centering Prayer or Lectio Divina, churches should have within their traditions ways of discerning together. At a minimum, your congregation can benefit from a team of those charged with deep listening in a time of change, perhaps called a Vision or Discernment Team. You can also embark on whole-congregation discernment. Depending on the size of your congregation, events such as Appreciative Inquiry Summits or Visioning Sessions can be helpful in giving voice to members' dreams for the future of your community. Such intentional focus and work by a small group of leaders or the whole congregation can temper any tendency toward reactivity and cultivate receptivity to where God may be calling us in the change.

Build healthy processes for organizational change (onboarding, retirements, structural/governance changes)

During change, we often find a spotlight on those areas in which our current systems and structures fall short. In my first experience with pastoral transition, I was a member in a congregation for the first time as an adult. The pastor had submitted their resignation so that they could leave to attend a rehabilitation program for addiction. The congregational bylaws required a congregational vote to accept a pastoral resignation. Beyond the strangeness of voting on whether someone had permission to leave a job, the congregational meeting preceding the vote became a mass therapy session for all those who had addiction in theirs or their family's history. During hour three of a meeting called immediately after worship (meaning no one had eaten in hours), one woman became overwhelmed and began shouting and crying. Finally, as if the outburst shook the gathered body into a realization of what they were doing, a member called the question and the congregation voted unanimously to accept the resignation. Needless to say, it was a trial by fire for me as a new member and highlighted the potential of a single line in the bylaws to bring about significant disruption and dysfunction.

Now is the time to review your bylaws to see if anything is a red flag for how your congregation will grapple with the change you are facing. It may require an external set of eyes from a consultant or denominational staff to spot things that may trip you up. If those red flags are present, it is time to make a change. While changing bylaws can seem intimidating, the prospect of a meeting like the one described above should spur you into action. Make sure, especially when your congregation is facing change, that your policies around people, processes, finances, and decision-making are those that promote healthy ways of relating for your church.

Celebrate!

Finally, celebrate when appropriate! With every ending comes a new beginning, and often those events are worth celebrating. In Chapter 5, I discuss how to use worship and rituals to mark and celebrate endings and new beginnings. Of course, there are other ways we celebrate as congregations.

Throw a party! If you are entering a new phase of ministry, launching a new program, moving to a new location, celebrate that in ways that are big and small. "Christen" the new thing with a bottle of champagne (or some non-alcoholic punch), cut a big red ribbon across the building doors, or hold an open house party. Invite members to write on index cards what they are most excited about and post the cards somewhere in the church building.

Be an evangelist and enthusiast. Use all your communications channels to acknowledge and celebrate whenever you can. Put up new banners or bulletin boards. Send out "birth announcements" about your new program. Create a YouTube video of members dancing or high fiving to say mission accomplished. Write newsletter articles and post on social media so even those who follow your congregation from afar can share in the experience of your transition.

When celebration, self-knowledge, healthy processes, and collective discernment are incorporated into the life of the congregation during a time of change, opportunities abound! The change will be more successful, and learning is more likely to occur. While intentional learning supports are another key aspect of finding transformation in times of change, and I will explore those further in the chapters ahead, using the model above will lay a foundation for your congregation to survive and even thrive in the face of whatever changes you are facing right now.

Reflection Questions:

- When is the last time your church threw a party to celebrate something new? What was the occasion?
- Do you have a group of people in your life to help you discern about big decisions?
- How well do members of your congregation know each other? How well do you all know those in the neighborhood around your church? What could help with that?

| 6 |

Changing Pastors and Changing Times at Suburban Presbyterian Church

Suburban Presbyterian Church sits next door to the courthouse in a former small town that now serves as a suburb to a major Southern city approximately 25 miles away. Suburban Presbyterian, in contrast to its neighbors, two red brick church buildings with white columns, is made of grey stone. The front is most notably framed by two notched turrets, one tall and one small, both containing gothic arched windows, flanking an arched center section that rises to a peak. The center section contains red doors and a round stained-glass window above. A brown sign with white lettering out front displays the name of the congregation. Although there is a ramp leading to this entry from the parking areas, very few people come and go through the red front doors. Occasionally, children and/or youth are present out front to hand out bulletins. More often, upon opening the doors to enter, an adult greeter approaches a visitor from inside the foyer to the sanctuary.

The red doors lead to a low-ceilinged foyer with several doors on various walls. Another set of doors ahead lead to the pale-yellow sanctuary with arched stuccoed walls. The side walls are paneled up to a chair rail with dark wood. On each side wall are several stained-glass windows, some bearing names in whose honor the windows were donated. Pews are dark wood, and chairs line the walls along the sides in short rows of 2-3 to expand the possible seating. There is an aisle down the center of the pews stretching from the entry doors to a raised front area, paneled with dark wood, that contains a pulpit, an altar, baptismal font, and banners interspersed with chairs and benches against the far wall. An American flag and a Christian flag stand on the far edges of the raised area. To the left of the raised area is a grand piano. Above all this, there is a large cross centered on sets of organ pipes framed by gothic arches. Adjoining the sanctuary is a three-story education building with a fellowship hall on the main floor and classrooms in the basement and top floor. Further down the block, a connected grey stone building contains of a vaulted multi-purpose space with additional classrooms in its basement.

On a typical Sunday, worship consists of announcements, traditional hymns and responsive prayers, scripture, a children's story, a sermon, and a time of offering. 80-100 people are typically in attendance. The congregation is predominantly white but does have a few members of color. The announcements at the beginning of the service are made in a casual and lighthearted manner, and a chiming of the hour after the announcements marks a turn to a more solemn and liturgical portion of the service containing readings, responsive prayers, and sung responses. Sermons return to a conversational feel, containing jokes and a warm presentation, but do at times contain contemporary and even controversial topics and challenges to the congregation. Hymns are mostly sung with enthusiasm. During the offering, visitors are asked to record their attendance on notepads in the pews. People disperse quickly after service unless there is a reception or other special event.

In addition to Sunday worship, Suburban celebrates and fellowships together at a reception for a departing staff member, adult discussions on Wednesday nights, and Wednesday night meals. The Wednesday night meals are free and open to all, as advertised on a sandwich board in front of the church. The meal is served in the large multi-purpose space. Food is ample and there was frequently a salad bar and dessert. Church members, with one gentleman taking lead, do most of the cooking and cleaning for the 30-70 adults and children in attendance. Following the Wednesday night meal, there are often adult discussions in the smaller fellowship hall with 10-20 primarily senior citizens in attendance. The discussions consist of a short talk by the pastor or other speaker, followed by questions and discussions. At all of these events, a warm, friendly welcome is offered by church members.

Suburban through the eyes of members

Sue, a retired white woman in her early 60s, has helped in various roles during her membership, and particularly enjoyed helping with the youth. Sue described Suburban as "a long-established church. We've celebrated our 150th anniversary in 2010, so now we're beyond that for almost five years. It's got a long history and pretty much a rich history, I think. It's small enough to accommodate the needs of the membership and large enough to address several needs of the community. That's the best part about the church. It's not too small and it's not too large. You don't get lost in the church, so to speak. It's a caring congregation. We're very supportive of each other. Most people know everybody else in the church, may not know names, but certainly know faces. It's more in line with the traditional Presbyterian Church than it is the modern, progressive church, you might say."

Jerry, a retired Black man in his late 50s, was a recent transplant to this suburban city and had found at Suburban a place of welcome and outreach to help with his needs, as well as opportunities for him to be of service. Jerry called Suburban, "one of the most giving, caring churches I've ever been associated with. The people are pretty much professional, and it's a church whose congregation extends generation to generation to generation. We have married couples in here that's been married 50 years. Not just one or two, a lot. A lot of senior citizens go here, and their grandkids go here, and their great-grandkids go here. It's one of the nicest, healthiest, caringest churches I've ever met."

Gregory and Alan, both white, both retired former business executives, have served the church on various councils and committees during their decades-long memberships. Gregory described Suburban as "a very loving, caring church. You can ask almost anybody who's capable if they will do [something], and they generally say yes. Because of our small population, our congregation, most everybody . . . About 50 of the congregation do most of the work." He mentioned that "[t]hose 50 usually have 3 to 5 jobs . . . so it makes it difficult to make significant changes." Alan served on the search committee in the congregation and had been active in working to create a cohesive church vision over the last few years. Alan observed that Suburban "has a long history going back to 1860 and, as you can see on the wall there, have had a lot of pastors over these years. It, to me, is a loving, caring church. We really think about serving people in need, and we have a lot of people in the congregation who are just what I call good people. They want to do things that we think Christ wants us to do . . . this church is a loving, caring church . . . Christ to me is the center of this church."

Suburban communicates in a variety of ways. The church provided documents in the form of emails, committee and session minutes, and emails and bulletins, many of which members cited as sources of information about the church. According to Jerry, "I look at the church bulletin. . . . and what they put up on the bulletin board." Sue explained further, "We do have bulletins that go out. There are things like e-mail communications. The Representative from the Session who heads the committees will report back to the committees. You know, it's a two-way street. The information goes in both directions. Then if there's a member who wants to bring something before the Session, then they will approach whoever . . . Like if it's a children's ministry thing, then they will approach the children's ministry and they in turn will report that and get things approved. It has to be officially sanctioned. . . ."
Longtime member Jim, a white man in his 70s who retired from a scientific field, expressed his concern that "We don't have the world's best website as far as being slick-looking, and it needs some help. We talk about getting it redesigned, but it does have all the basic information

about the activities. You can bring up a calendar of events and it's all there."

Big changes and big issues

Late one September, the pastor of Suburban Presbyterian announced his retirement. Members of Suburban describe learning about the pastor leaving through an announcement in church. Sue remembered, "He made the announcement in church, I think. There was rumor beforehand that he might be. There were some people who maybe knew in advance of the announcement."

Pulpit supply pastors were hired to preach until an interim pastor could be located. By November 2013, an interim had been located and begun serving. The interim pastor fulfilled all the duties of a pastor and guided the Session, or governing board of the church, on how to go about a pastor search and what a timeline for a search might look like. During his tenure, the interim pastor preached, led staff and lay leader teams and committees, visited members, and led the church in several small group studies, including one focused on discerning the church's mission in the community going forward.

The church was also grappling with the issue of same-sex marriage during its transition. The national and state denominational bodies had voted to change their policy on same-sex marriage. The interim pastor informed the congregation about the change and how it came about and organized an informational session with a local pastor who had been a voting member of the national body when the decision was made. Several interviewees reported spending extensive time researching and working on their church's response to this change. Gregory and Jim both became deeply involved in the congregational engagement with the issue. In the end, the congregation's Session voted, in a close vote, to prevent any same-sex marriages from occurring in the church building or on the grounds. In Presbyterian polity, the church cannot forbid a pastor from following their conscience on any matter. However, interviewees who served on the search committee were clear that they intended to communicate that position to any pastor candidates and that they felt it was important that the new pastor be of the same mind as the congregation regarding this issue.

A Pastor Nominating Committee was elected four months after the pastor's retirement. Sue described the work of the church during transition this way, "The church is given a period in which decide upon the new minister. We decide who is called to the church. Likewise, whoever comes has to feel the calling as well." The following May, they completed a ministry information form that would inform prospective pastors about their church and their needs. Over the year and a half that the committee searched before I concluded this research, they reviewed numerous files and sermons from potential pastors, interviewed several pastor candidates, and offered the pastor position to several candidates, as well as to the interim pastor. When I concluded this research, none of those candidates had accepted the call, and the search committee had returned to reviewing information on candidates to identify additional prospects.

Alan pointed to a particularly frustrating piece of information he received, "we thought we had somebody, and then we found out the spouse didn't want to live in this area, so you spend all that time with that person and then find out, well, that's not going to work." He said this increased the difficulty in finding a pastor for their church, despite much hard work. "The point I'm trying to make is that trying to find the right pastor for this congregation obviously is difficult because we have worked at it. These people on this search committee have worked that hard trying to find somebody. They've interviewed a lot of people. They've looked at a lot of resumes, a lot of things, but still no result. . . . We're still looking for a pastor. We've been through a long time of looking and trying to find the right person. A lot of people applied. A lot of screening has been done. A lot of looking. Still, though, we don't have anyone for one reason or another. Hopefully we will find somebody soon."

Due to the length of the transition, the interim pastor's term was extended three times. However, after serving a year and a month, the Interim Pastor announced that he had served the term agreed on for his interim along with additional extensions of that time and needed to leave to take another interim call. Pulpit supply pastors were hired to preach for a few weeks until a new interim began serving the congregation a few months later. Suburban went through additional staff changes during their extended pastoral transition, including hiring a new children's minister and administrative assistant and the retirement of the music minister.

It took over two years for Suburban to call their next settled pastor.

| 7 |

Embracing Change

Beyond the basics presented in the previous chapter for tackling unexpected changes as they arise, becoming intentional about learning and transformation during transition can equip congregants to better handle change whenever it comes. If any form of church is to survive into the future, Christians who can handle change and harness it for real learning and transformation will be crucial to that survival. Congregations are the contexts that can develop such change-ready Christians. Those ready to face change and transition with open minds and tools for learning will lay the foundation for Christianity to survive and thrive in the coming years, decades, and beyond.

So, how can we build our congregational life in ways that help our congregations move beyond merely a successful transition into true transformation for the congregation?

- Confess discomfort with change.
- Use stories of change from your faith tradition.
- Learn about our reactions to change.
- Build support systems.
- Cultivate reflection.

Confession

To grow during times of change, we must acknowledge, I might even say confess, our discomfort with change. We are all planners. We may not be particularly good ones, but we all do it. We envision what is ahead for us, and we start thinking about how we will navigate that future. We have dreams and hopes for that future, and we paint vivid pictures of that future in our minds. But of course, things do not always go as planned.

And one of the hardest types of change for us to handle is when life makes us take such a radical detour that it completely upends all those plans. When life interrupts what we had thought our future would be. We get laid off from a job that we loved, or we find that we hate the job we always wanted. A significant relationship ends through death or a breakup, or we realize that a significant life partnership is not likely for us. We have an unexpected pregnancy, or we find that we cannot have children. We have a health crisis that limits our activities or devastates our savings, or a family member's health forces us into full time caregiving. Our church goes through an organizational crisis or loses a long-serving pastor. There are so many ways our life and future can refuse to turn out as we had planned.

Molly Baskette, in her book *Standing Naked before God*, addresses our need to tell our stories to people who are present to the possibility of really knowing us. Her church practiced confessing to each other regularly in worship, preparing and telling stories of their sins and vulnerabilities and what came next. Doing so trained the congregation in understanding and practicing that no aspect of ourselves should be left out of our practice of faith. Baskette cites Henri Nouwen's call for us to "put our wounds into the service of others."[17] We may not know who might be healed in the hearing of it if we share our stories of crisis and change, and how we responded, good or bad. We can know that the collective will be transformed by this radical act of presence and witness, every time.

In the recent past and even now, some churches called such a practice testimony. While our modern congregations do not require us to testify to a salvation experience that passes muster before being accepted into membership, testimony in a more general sense still has the power to transform. An opportunity to practice testimony is included in the Church After Small Group Curriculum in the Appendix, along with additional resources that can help you build this practice into the ongoing life of your congregation.

Sacred Stories

To build change into our understanding of faith, we must weave stories of change into our practice of faith. There are numerous stories in the Bible about journeys through unexpected change. Do we tell those stories enough? When we tell them, do we facilitate reflection on how we might face unexpected change in our faith journeys? Abraham is commanded by God, "Go from your country and your kindred and your father's house to the land that I will show you."[18] He thought he would live out the rest of his days in Ur. He was already elderly. But Abraham went anyway.

Moses hears from God, "I am the Lord; tell Pharaoh king of Egypt all that I am speaking to you."[19] He responded by calling himself a "nobody" and doubted he could do such a thing. God told him again and again that he was the one to speak. Moses went anyway.

Ruth followed her mother-in-law to a new land to ensure she was cared for. Naomi told her not to come. Ruth would be a foreigner in this new land, a stranger to all but Naomi. Ruth went anyway.

Jesus' movement was grounded in story. Jesus came and told a new story about God's relationship with humanity, a different story than the governmental or religious authorities of his time. Brian McLaren says that for organizing religion, words are important, but even more important are stories.[20] McLaren also observes that in the foundational stories of Christian faith, humans, and Jesus, are constantly on the move, in transition. The stories Jesus and his followers told along the way, their public theology, cast a compelling vision for where they were headed.

Such stories have a way of cultivating our moral imagination, or our capacity to bring creative futures to life.[21] While the world tells stories of domination and fear, we can tell stories of creativity and hope from the Bible or from the lives of our congregation and/or its members. This kind of storytelling happens on Sunday mornings or at other gatherings of your faith community.

We must tell such stories beyond our church walls as well. The only way to bring new people into the story is to tell it to them. You can share new stories of walking through change on social media and in conversation with neighbors. Perhaps you will record stories of hope and distribute them through a podcast or other medium. You may write letters to the editor or submit a column to your local paper.

If you tell the stories of how change is an essential part of spiritual journeys, your congregation will not only internalize this embrace of change but help others in their orbit grapple with changes they face in their lives as individuals and in organizations. Talk about good news!

Increasing Understanding

To build our change skills, we must grow our understanding of how we respond to change. We do not hear much about the internal journeys of the folks in the Bible, but we certainly know how it feels when such an unexpected change happens to us. We almost always respond negatively at first. Our own brains are responsible for much of our negative reactions to unexpected change. Science has found that as we go throughout our daily routines, our brains anticipate the next most likely event. Most of the time, this serves us well, saving us time and energy in navigating our lives and world.[22]

Unfortunately, when that next most likely event does not occur, our brain begins secreting strong chemicals that make us extra alert and ready to act. These chemicals make us feel on edge and uncomfortable, training us to dislike unexpected change. To get through this feeling, we start to sort through this unexpected event and try to categorize it. In truly unexpected life changes this can be difficult, and our brains begin to exist in a state of uncertainty, which we experience as fear or anxiety. We start to assign labels of threat or blame.[23] We feel out of control. As humans, we thrive when we have a sense of control. Some things in our lives will never be self-chosen. Illness, job loss, death of a loved one. And research also suggests that the more we feel that life events are out of our control, the less positive action we are likely to take.

Mice, in a seemingly random situation where there is no way to predict whether they will receive a shock or some cheese, eventually become listless and just lay there without taking any action at all.[24] People who experience a negative career shock, such as downsizing or transfer to an unwanted location, were actually less likely to take positive action on improving skills through graduate training.[25] Unfortunately, the more we are shocked by negative life events, the less likely we can be to shape our lives through positive choices. The challenge is getting past feeling out-of-control and fearful so that we can move toward reorientation into a new understanding.

Thankfully, this sort of disorientation is actually a key factor in our transformation. Transformational learning only occurs in the context of disorientation. One of our key tasks in congregations is helping members understand that these feelings are part of the process. Like grief, the only way to get through it is to go through it. When we avoid these feelings, cover them up with dysfunctional behaviors or try to skip past them, we fail to learn and be transformed. But if we are trained to expect these feelings and how to respond, we may be able to sit with the discomfort long enough to learn.

What does this mean for congregations? Training our congregations on change and supporting our members in times of change is not only compassionate but necessary. Understanding, community, and support are the best counters for fear and feeling a lack of control.

Supporting Each Other

To avoid resistance or getting stuck in times of change, we must build support systems to carry us through. We sometimes hear negative messages about change from our peers: that change is bad and means either hard work ahead or is a sign of failure or defeat. Unexpected change is frequently seen by us and by others as bad news. It can be hard to share an unexpected change with those in our lives because we fear their reaction. Often these changes are quite tangled up with our shame that things are not rolling along as planned for us anymore. Others' reactions, no matter how well-meaning, can serve to reinforce this shame. People seek to help us figure out where we went wrong or tell us stories of even worse things that happened to them or someone they knew.

This applies in church transitions as well. Those who previously would have invited others to church are more hesitant without a settled pastor or when a church changes locations. Depending on the reason for the transition, members may feel ashamed and reluctant to share the story with friends and family.

We are not unique in experiencing unhelpful friends and family during times of change. In the biblical story of Job, after he loses his wealth, his family, his health, friends ask him if he deserved all this for something bad he had done, ask him if he could stop dwelling on his misfortune, and ask him how he could be so greedy as to want all his wealth back. How many of us have heard reactions like this from friends and family when dealing with an unexpected life change? All this is grounded in labeling the event as "bad news." Yet we never really know what will come from a big change, whether a personal change or a community change such as pastoral transition.

If your church has not already developed a robust system for caring for each other as members within a supportive web of community, it is not too late. Examples of such systems include Stephen Ministries, Deacons, and/or small groups. The Church After Curriculum in the Appendix provides one way to get started with small groups that learn about change together while supporting one another while facing a particular change. This is not the only model that will work, but the more your congregation members can rely on others in their community to understand the gifts of change and support them during seasons of change, the greater their learning and transformation will be.

Taking Time

To deepen our learning, we must find the pause in the midst of change. There is an old parable that goes like this:

> A farmer lost his horse. All his neighbors said: "How awful!" But the farmer simply replied: "Could be bad, could be good, don't know yet." Then the horse returned with a stallion. Now the neighbors said: "How wonderful for you!" But the farmer replied: "Could be bad, could be good, don't know yet." A few days later the farmer's son was riding the stallion. He fell off and broke his leg. Once again, the neighbors chimed in: "That's terrible news!" But the farmer just told them: "Could be bad, could be good, don't know yet." That weekend the country went to war, and the generals went from village to village taking young men to fight in the war. They did not take the farmer's son since his leg was broken. The neighbors all expressed how lucky the farmer was that his son had broken his leg, since now he did not have to go to war and risk being killed. But the farmer simply said: "Could be bad, could be good, don't know yet."[26]

It can be almost impossible to reserve judgment about unexpected change in our lives. But as we see in this parable, it is impossible to know the full consequences of something unexpected until we get much further down the road. The challenge of big changes is that our own judgments and the judgments of others cloud our ability to find the right path through change or find those areas where we can take back some control through acceptance, action, or ritual. Yet we must push through our unhelpful brain reactions toward just those things. Unexpected and seemingly random change is in fact embedded in living as human beings, despite our perceptions of control and predictability. And if we recognize that our pursuits of control may actually keep us from God's calling, what can really help us navigate unexpected change?

One way is to practice Sabbath. Sabbath, in ancient Israel, was both the practice of resting one day a week but also practices of letting land rest, forgiving debts, and acting in sustainable ways with others in the community. The word sustainable is key here. A congregation that seeks to sustain itself over time must navigate change. Pauses like the practice of Sabbath cushion change in ways that make congregations more sustainable.

Ross L. Smillie observes that modern Sabbath observance can serve as a formative practice when people and communities remember to think beyond economics, marketing, social pressures, consumption, and frantic activity as indicators of success. Time away from this pressure shows that other ways of living are not only possible but joyful, life-giving, and desirable.[27]

When does your congregation take time to pause its activity to rest and imagine alternatives? If you are anything like the churches I have known and loved, it is not on Sunday mornings during the busy rush of worship and educational activities. I challenge you to find a week very soon where your church can pause, halting all normal activities for a time of prayer and rest. For smaller pauses, build times of silence and reflection into your worship life. The next chapter and the Appendix provide ideas for incorporating reflection on change into your worship services and events. You might be surprised by the possibilities you find in your congregation's collective imagination when activity slows down a bit.

I hope not all of this is new to your practice of faith. But if it is, add in a bit at a time until you can say that your church embraces change intentionally and holistically. If your congregation provides opportunities to confess experiences with change, tell sacred stories about change, teach and learn about human reactions to change, support members in times of change, and pause and reflect, you will be much more likely to find transformation in the change that you are facing.

Reflection Questions:

- What is your favorite Bible Study about change?

- Have you tried a Sabbath practice when dealing with changes in your life? What was that like?
- When does your congregation take time to pause its activity to rest?

| 8 |

Urban Congregational Church: "survival mode"

Urban Congregational Church meets in a non-traditional setting for a church, just inside the metro area of a major U.S. city in the Southeast U.S. Their church building is single-story, constructed of stucco and concrete block, formerly a store, along a commercial stretch of a highway between the city and its Eastern suburbs. There is a lighted sign out front elevated on a pole, similar to nearby business signage. The five-lane highway that it fronts takes drivers from the Downtown area out to the encircling highway and beyond to additional suburbs and exurbs. Near the church are a CVS pharmacy, several convenience stores, a liquor store, a vet, some auto mechanics, and several low-rise office buildings and apartment complexes.

Upon entering the clear glass front doors flanked by two full height clear windows, a station of candles is off to the left, and a solid wall covers part of the room directly in front of the entrance. On this wall is an assemblage of cloth and items appearing as an altar of sorts, as well as a cross. On the other side of the dividing wall, the sanctuary contains an elevated audio-visual workspace at the rear, and rows of chairs on the diagonal divided by a center aisle facing a raised stage at the front, flanked by an organ on the left and piano on the right. Overhead on the left is a multimedia screen. At the far wall behind the stage, the wall is covered with shimmering cloth and multiple banners expressing the religious season.

On arriving, a church visitor is usually greeted inside the doors by a member with a bulletin. Small groups of members are often gathered in conversation in the time before worship. The congregation is multiracial. Children, though only 2-3 are occasionally in attendance, are present for the entire service. Weekly Sunday worship consists of readings, songs, prayers, a sermon, and communion. A somewhat liturgical style and adherence to the lectionary texts is blended with some music in a more contemporary style. The use of a screen projecting images and lyrics adds a contemporary touch. Most music is accompanied by piano, with occasional use of guitar and, very rarely, the organ. Readers appear to include both clergy and laity, as do communion servers. Readings are done from the lectern on the platform, or occasionally the lectern and the pulpit, if there are two readers. The sermon is preached from the pulpit. During communion, served every Sunday, congregants often come up for communion together as couples or family units and are then gathered into an embrace by the servers and prayed for by the clergy member of the pair. After worship, members visit with one another, primarily in the worship area, although coffee and refreshments are available in the social hall.

Urban members and guests also gather for congregational forums, social events, and celebrations. Congregational forums are typically led by members of the governing board, and members can ask questions of the board members or supply their perspectives on issues under discussion. Social events are held in the fellowship hall or at a local restaurant, and are jovial and light-hearted, even at times a bit bawdy. After the Supreme Court ruling legalizing same sex marriage in the United States, members gathered in the fellowship hall for celebration and conversation. Members applauded joyfully and shared reflections on what this change would mean for their lives, with many announcing upcoming wedding plans.

Urban through the eyes of members

Member Sarah describes Urban as "Progressive, definitely progressive. . . . It is a real blend of people from people who are both theologically . . . conservative, and positive to people who are known in the community as activists, LGBT activists, and they tend to be more liberal in their theology. Then, we have a heritage, a history of inclusive language." Another member, Allyson, described Urban this way: "It's small because we originally started as the MCC. It's mostly a lesbian congregation, a small, gay group of men and then a few straight people, a few families. I'd say that's the demographic of the church . . . Even in churches where I would say they are very progressive, . . . you had to abide by those rules . . . there's always that little bit of, 'We're at church. We can't say this. We can't do this.' You just don't get that [at Urban]. . . . People are just who they are."

Inclusivity is evident in Urban"s membership and its approach to ministry. Sarah, an older white woman in her 70s and Urban member for several decades, serves in a lay minister role at Urban, helping with pastoral care and worship. Mark, a young black man in his early 30s, had attended seminary and had been seeking his first pastorate while serving in various capacities, first in the small church that was merging with Urban and now at Urban. Frank, a white man in later middle age, was a member of the small church that was in the process of merging with Urban. Allyson, a white woman in her late 30s, had served in various roles on Urban"s governing board over the last few years. Gail, a young black woman in her late 20s, had recently become more involved at Urban and currently serves on at least one team dealing with planning for the future of the church. Wendy, a young Asian woman in her 20s, was a fairly new member of Urban and participated primarily in worship and social events.

The members see Urban as notable in its inclusivity and family-like connections between members. Gail said Urban is, "an inclusive place as far as the people who are there. . . . There's not much (racial) diversity, but at the same time they're open to it. It just feels welcoming, and it's a place where they're Catholics or people who aren't quite sure where they stand as far as spirituality and religion goes or whether or not they're spiritual but not religious. . . . it's this place where things can evolve. It's open to questions and respecting, I think, everyone's different point of view and trying to offer a different experience to kind of serve everyone." According to Wendy, "it's a very close-knit group. Even when new people come in, it doesn't take that long before they're part of the family. Having grown up in church, I would say when people describe the church as a family, I think our church definitely fits that." Wendy went on to say, "they're so welcoming there. It's not shove it down your throat religion, beliefs, and everything. They're so understanding. I've mentioned, I'm totally down for volunteering, but I don't know anything about the bible. Nothing, literally nothing. That's what I like about it. . . . It's not always traditional setting for a church, so I feel comfortable there, I don't feel intimidated. . . . They're very accommodating in the sense of inclusive, trying to include all people. Any differences you have, religious, physical ability, gender, . . . orientation."

Wendy has a disability that requires some assistance for transportation to the church. She says, "They're always willing to help out, accessible, they're always so open minded to me, they're always keeping me in mind." Gail pointed out personal communications such as emails and phone calls from Urban Congregational and its members as a frequent source of information. "I think it's just them communicating, mostly after church, the service, like that time that we have or through email or if they have your number then they'll call you and want to have a conversation about it so it's pretty . . . there's a lot of communication that goes on and easy to find out if you . . . engage." These tendencies towards personal communication and one-on-one assistance contribute to the family atmosphere.

A surprising departure

Urban took a more unconventional path through transition that echoed its history of breaking through traditional restrictions on the Christian faith. In late fall, the pastor of Urban announced that she would be leaving as of the end of the year. A meeting followed worship to allow members to ask questions and discuss. Members remember when the pastor's departure was announced. Sarah recalled, "someone on the board said I want you to be prepared. She is going to resign. The board got notice on Friday night at 10:30. They were in session all day on Saturday, and she announced her leaving on Sunday." Gail remembered the day she learned the pastor was leaving, "It was at church, and she announced it, I think it was after and then they took questions and stuff, opened it up for people who had questions. [The pastor] left because she wanted people to be open and ask what they wanted and say what they wanted and so she decided to go to let that happen. . . . . . . [They asked questions like] Why? What's going to happen? Who? Are we going to hire another pastor? How long? . . . Are we going to continue having church on Sundays? You know, service, are we going to continue having church on Sunday? Service, is it going to stop? . . . a lot of people were upset, crying." Wendy remembered, "I don't know the politics truly behind it, but I know that [the pastor who was leaving] had said, 'Hey, I want to let you guys know that I've got this opportunity in Tennessee. It's my calling, I need to do it.' . . . In my opinion, I was like, 'Okay, may the force be with you.' I looked to my left, and all of a sudden people were in tears. Of course, they had been there for a while. That's how I found out."

A few weeks later, the church held a meeting after worship to discuss the future of the church. From there, those members involved in the governing board had to determine the next steps after the pastor's departure. Allyson described that time, ". . . [existing staff said], 'Here's what I'll have to do.' . . . We were definitely working with our conference minister and her explaining what are our options . . . if we [weren't going to use existing staff] before we made that decision." Allyson remembered one decision in detail, and the thought processes behind it. "We chose to not have [the outgoing pastor] serve out her two months. . . . She gave us the two months' notice. We just went ahead and paid her out for that two months and did not have her. We had her come back for 1 service where everybody could say goodbye and bring closure to it."" She says that the problem necessitating that decision was that ""the Sunday that she resigned, she was leaving either that day or the next day to go [abroad] for two weeks. Then she was going to be away for professional development for another week. For the first three weeks of that two months and then we were going to hit Advent." Allyson described how they considered their next steps, saying that "We didn't want to have Advent being, *This one is going away. This is really sad.* Given that she was already not going to be there basically for 3 weeks." Looking back at that decision, she said, "It just made sense."

A few months after the pastor's departure, the governing board held a congregational forum to discuss the budget and other issues facing the church. After another month of discernment, the congregation decided to install the former staff responsible for worship and administration into a licensed minister position and arranged to have her alternate preaching with one of the leaders of the other small church, utilizing other lay and ordained members and leaders to help with worship and other programs. They held a special worship service to mark this change in leadership.

A possible merger

A few months later, another congregation, New Way Church, had begun discussing the possibility of consolidating with Urban. This congregation was small and young and had been led by two planting pastors and a group of lay and ordained volunteer leaders. Mark described New Way as, "a funky, granola congregation. Eclectic, contemporary worship, great music. We have this live jazz band with this R&B, jazz-flavored pianist and drums and Led Zeppelin-like guitar player, and it is just really soulful and funky and fresh and new. With the merge [with Urban], it's a fusion of a very, I wouldn't say high liturgical but more traditional church with the funky, fresh, eclectic bunch."

After years of meeting in various locations around the city, New Way had discerned the possibility of joining with a settled congregation and approached Urban about that possibility. Members of this small congregation were attending Urban during the research period, and a Consolidation Committee had been formed to formalize this relationship. Sarah said, "They needed a place to be, and they had sought to be with or use the property of [Urban in its previous location] but . . . . . . it just wasn't enough yet. [Then our licensed minister] really had the idea when she talked to [one of their leaders] that it might be a good thing for us to just worship together rather than try to be two different separate things, but we didn't really want it to be a merger. We wanted it to be a blend of both congregations. I think that we've done that pretty well because we brought in elements of things that they did in their worship into our worship."

Allyson recalled, "we had their members come worship with us to introduce them and see if their style of worship might work with our style of worship . . . . . .We do tend to do the same thing every Sunday, much more structured, less interactive than what they were doing. They came. We liked them. They liked us. They decided they wanted to join with us." Sarah described the situation, ""I think that at this time, we're a blend. I think we have moved from the survival mode to now, how do we get this thing going. . . . I believe we are a small church. In some respects, we look like a storefront, but we really aren't. . . . There's a spirit of let's do this together, let's make it happen.""

The Consolidation Committee continued work on bylaws and other procedural aspects of the process. Beyond the formalities of consolidation, there were challenges in integrating the two congregations. Sarah observed that the complete blending of the congregations was taking time. She said, "There's still work to be done, because they still sit with each other, and there's only a beginning of them coming to our social events."

The following months and years were difficult for the congregation. Despite the consolidation bringing two small congregations into one organization, budgetary restraints meant they had to leave their space for another in a converted house in a suburb farther from the city. They were now meeting 9 miles, almost half an hour in traffic, from their prior location. The difficulties of this move and the lack of funding to hire a full time settled pastor led to further declines in attendance and engagement.

Within two years of their multiple transitions, Urban Congregational ended its life as a worshiping community.

| 9 |

Practicing Change

Transformation is possible in every transition of our lives. However, too often, we grapple with these changes without support or guidance, and too often, are left unchanged or changed in negative ways by those experiences. What if every person experiencing a profound change in their lives had a community of support and guidance so that through that experience, they might be transformed for the better? If that were the case, we might find ourselves more receptive and optimistic in times of change, knowing our community had our back. We might rest in the knowledge and hope that change is necessary to help us become all that we were created to be. What a wonderful possibility!

I have good news: The church can serve as just that community of support and guidance for each of its members. By building strategies and structures that support members during times of congregational change, the church will be ready and able to also support them through all the changes of their lives.

There are four principles that research shows to be most important in becoming transformed by transitions in our lives:

- Acceptance
- Mindfulness
- Ritual
- Community

We can build these principles into the lives of our churches so that our members can find transformation in times of change.

Acceptance

To begin the work of transformation, we can develop one of the most powerful personal responses to change: acceptance. In the *I Ching*, an ancient wisdom text from China, also known as "The Book of Changes," we find this passage:

> "It is only when we have the courage to face things exactly as they are, without any self-deception or illusion, that a light will develop out of events, by which the path to success may be recognized."[28]

The field of psychology also emphasizes the importance of acceptance in facing a changed future. A recent addition to the menu of possibilities for people using therapy to cope with life's changes is Dialectical Behavioral Therapy, or DBT. At its core is radical acceptance, which makes a clear distinction between pain and suffering.[29] Pain is a part of life, but fighting against that pain is the source of much suffering. Radical acceptance is the way to peace.

A painful reality generally causes us to want to rail against it. Yet DBT argues that real change can only come from a radical, or a full and non-judgmental, acceptance. Not condoning or being ok with something that happens to us that seems unfair or too hard but accepting that it simply is.[30]

Mark, from Urban Congregational, tells this story about the attitudes of congregational leaders toward change, "I was doing worship. I was going to preach that Sunday, I had everything kind of honed out. I also was talking to a board member, . . . and they were very clear that things had been always done a specific way." He began to interpret this through the lens of his experience in social work, "I think the average bear went in and got really defensive. . . . In that moment my clinician hat just kind of, this person's really scared and they really need me to reassure them that a different way is okay. I just had to really step outside of myself and just kind of say you know, I really get this change is not easy for you and that having new people in this space is something that you want, but doing things differently because people are in this space, it can be uncomfortable for some. I need you to trust me enough to let me try this and know that everything will be okay. They had their judgments and their opinions, impressions about the way they wanted it, but you know, they went with it and had faith in me."

He told of his belief in the necessity of faith, to leave room for God in the process. "I think people get so fixated, myself included, on things being a certain way. There is no room for the Holy Spirit to come in and do what needs to be done. How can God really take hold of this space, and the dam breaks and people come in and be their authentic selves and embrace their gifts and vitality really happen if you're so fixated on things being a certain way?"

You may recognize a parallel here with Christian scriptures that call us toward a peace that passes our understanding. We can also draw on Christ's example of helping the disciples accept his fate, as he faced the final days of his life. Radical acceptance necessarily involves emotions such as grief or sadness. But fully experiencing those emotions moves us through them into future paths of action. Rather than a cycle of fighting or railing against the reality, which keeps us from real progress, we are freed by accepting a new reality and letting go of the old to choose our most healthy responses to the new.[31]

Mindfulness

Developing a practice of mindfulness or meditation is another way we can increase our capacity for acceptance. Mindfulness is the practice of being aware of our experiences in the moment without judging those experiences. Research shows that we can increase our mindfulness through intentional practices.[32] Increasing our mindfulness changes our brain patterns in ways that can be measured through brain scanning, literally transforming our neural responses. This change in neural responses reduces our emotional reactivity, increases our skills for flexible thinking, and dampens those brain reactions to unexpected events which keep us off balance and unable to move forward.[33]

When Jesus was facing transitions in his life and ministry, he withdrew for times of prayer, away from the crowds. This can serve as an example for us to take time for mindfulness in our own lives when change seems all around us.

Ritual

We can also find growth in changes when we allow ourselves time and space for ritual as we turn from our old road onto the new. This ritual may look like saying goodbye to a place or community that has served us well but cannot be with us on our new road. It may look like acknowledging those parts of ourselves that we must leave behind. It may also look like celebrating and blessing the experiences that will come on this new road, recognizing that God is in it all.

In *The Wild Edge of Sorrow: Rituals of Renewal and the Sacred Work of Grief*, Francis Weller suggests that "We are creatures of ritual. We have been using rituals for tens of thousands of years. There is something about ritual that resonates deep in the bone. It is a 'language older than words,' relying not so much on speech as on gestures, rhythms, movements, and emotion." He quotes author and ritual facilitator Z. Budapest as saying, "The purpose of ritual is to wake up the old mind in us, to put it to work. The old ones inside us, the collective unconscious, the many lives, the different eternal parts, the senses and parts of the brain that have been ignored. Those parts do not speak English. They do not care about television. But they do understand candlelight and colors. They do understand nature."[34]

Weller also asserts that ritual repairs our souls, helping us remember and reestablish our inner rhythms and to place them once again in accord with the deeper cadence of our soul.[35] In other words, rituals help us encounter the difficulties in our lives in ways that are potentially transformative. Rituals help us move *from* feeling stuck *toward* new directions.

Rituals have been shown to be helpful in alleviating grief, reducing anxiety, and increasing confidence. This is true even when people claim that they do not believe rituals work. In experiments, scientists found that rituals gave people a greater sense of acceptance, and that such a sense of control reduced feelings of grief. Most of the rituals they studied were personal, not religious or community-based, involving things like writing on a paper and tearing it up or destroying old photographs. Any ritual, it seems, will do, even an arbitrary one designed by the scientists, to help increase a sense of acceptance and control after an unexpected loss. Rituals can look like communion at church or burning old papers from the life we are leaving behind, or scattering stones in a stream. No matter the ritual, God is there with us as we remember, grieve, celebrate, or bless.

Community

Once we use tools like reflection, mindfulness, and ritual to accept our new direction, then what? Community can support us through change, and particularly in times of transitions that affect the whole community, can be invaluable for our transformation.

With our community, we can take a fearless inventory of our own calls from God and the internal and external resources that we still have that will be most helpful for our new journey. Then, we can begin noticing what gifts, talents, and resources are present in our community, and simply ask one another if we are willing to share. What do we each need for this change that we do not possess? Who has this gift, or passion, or knowledge? How can we ask them for it?

This asking can be the most difficult step of all. If we needed a European power adapter for a trip overseas, we might not hesitate to ask a friend who had recently been to Europe. But if we need to borrow some resilience, or some positive attitude, or help navigating the job market, we often forget to ask for just what we need. Often all we need to do is ask to get what we need, and as a bonus, this strengthens our relationships and support systems.

We need support and companions on our journeys. These relationships and connections will sustain us when our new road is long and exhausting.

Building these practices into the life of your church

Now that we know what people need to be supported and transformed in their time of transition, how can we build these structures and practices into our community of faith? We can be thoughtful and strategic about building these principles into the whole life of our congregation, not just during times of active change, but in all seasons of the life of the church.

Radical Acceptance

Although the roots of radical acceptance come from Buddhism and psychology, there are many ways in which this concept resonates with a Christian faith. First, it echoes the idea that God loves us just as we are, even as we are called by God to take actions of love and justice. The world is not as it should be but is loved and accepted as it is. Second, we hear in scripture to "Be still and know that I am God." This is often used as a meditation or prayer and can be a powerful touchstone for the power of remaining still and accepting the reality of our lives before taking further action.

Tara Brach, in her book *Radical Acceptance*, suggests practices for groups or individuals that can help with learning this practice.[37] These include quiet periods of guided reflection and meditation. Some echo ancient prayer practices rooted in the Christian tradition. Many of these can be easily adapted to a church setting, particularly if a spiritual director is available to facilitate, as spiritual direction often includes learning to radically accept one's place on their spiritual path before taking steps in any forward direction.

Mindfulness

Mindfulness, another practice whose roots are often traced in origin to Eastern Philosophies, is also easily adapted to a Christian context. Although ignored for many centuries, mindfulness through contemplative prayer and meditation has been a part of Christianity since its beginnings. Ancient church fathers and mothers spent hours in prayer and meditation in hopes of finding God's spirit within themselves, retreating to caves or deserts in pursuit of the elusive essence of faith. Many modern churches have begun to have regular opportunities for such prayer or meditation, including practicing Lectio Divina, centering prayer, body prayer, and other prayer practices that increase mindfulness of self and faith. If no one in your church feels confident to take on leading such an effort, spiritual directors, again, have often been trained in some or all these Christian practices of mindfulness and can be retained to facilitate them in your congregation.

Ritual

Churches would seemingly be rife with opportunities for ritual, yet too often the only rituals we practice in our congregations are occasional baptisms, communion, and funerals. What a missed opportunity! Churches in the midst of a change can use rituals to celebrate the past and bless a new opportunity to do God's work in a new way. Transitioning churches can use rituals to publicly pray for, bless, and consecrate the season of change. Rituals can help members feel the sadness of the ending if they write their favorite memories on a stone and cast it into the water. Rituals can help members embrace their hopes for the future by allowing them to speak these hopes into the sacred space of worship, rather than just answer a survey or participate in a brainstorming session.

All of these and rituals specific to and designed for each congregation and its needs are available, with the only resources needed being a little creativity and openness to experimentation. Gathering a group of interested people to plan and write liturgy for such rituals is another way to engage members more deeply into both the transition process and the life of the church.

Sharing Gifts and Strengthening Community

Churches would seemingly be experts at creating community and sharing gifts among their members. However, churches over the centuries have increasingly echoed our individualistic and consumeristic Western culture where it is "every man (and woman) for themselves." Often church members are not even aware of the many gifts, talents, and passions that occupy the pews alongside them every Sunday. A change is a prime opportunity to remedy that if this work has not already been undertaken.

Churches can lead members in interviewing each other to build an inventory of people and their gifts and strengthen connections between members. Once this work is done, providing a bit of matchmaking for members with similar gifts and passions to connect, and providing opportunities, such as a time bank, for people to ask for those gifts and talents they may need from their fellow members, can further strengthen the community in your congregation.[38] This kind of sharing and asking also helps members learn to be vulnerable with one another. A strong, collaborative community that promotes vulnerability is essential for transformative learning from change.

With all these practices integrated into the life of our community, we can be sure that our members are fully supported during times of change for our church or in other areas of their lives. We can also rest in the hope that these tools will transform them, and with them, our congregation, into Christians who face change with the understanding that God is co-creating them even during challenging transitions. These change-ready Christians can be voices of hope and light in their families, workplaces, and other organizations as they experience change in those contexts. Rather than living into the stereotype of Christians who resist change at all costs, they can carry into those spaces the Christian hope that change can be a positive thing, for each of us and for our world.

Reflection Questions:

- Does your church have rituals for times of change?
- How do your members support each other during congregational change?
- What might it shift if your church cultivated radical acceptance?

| 10 |

Helping Children and Youth with Change

In some ways, children can seem more adaptable than adults. They experience change every year when they transition from one grade or school to the next. Many children find their families changing through the addition of siblings or parental divorce or marriage. Others move across states and even countries as their parents take new jobs or return to school.

In other ways, though, children are supported by routines. So anything that changes those routines can be challenging. In church life, children can easily become accustomed to the routine of their religious education and the familiar faces of the church leaders who guide them. Whether it is an unexpected change due to crisis, a seasonal transition of Sunday School teachers due to the changing lives of volunteers, or a transition in staff that work with children and youth or lead in worship, children do notice and are impacted by these changes. Just as with adults, this can become an opportunity to help children build skills for transition and change that will help them throughout their lives.

What practices are most helpful for teaching children about transition and change?

Congregational transitions can be an ideal time to begin building change skills in children and youth. The following tips and ideas may help you develop programming for children in your congregation around issues of change.

Explain things truthfully in a way that children can understand. Depending on their age, they may become aware fairly quickly from adult conversations and behavior that something big is going on in the life of the church. Tell them what is happening once it becomes public knowledge. Explain that leaders, just like other grownups, do not keep one job or volunteer role forever, and that a new leader will come soon. Explain that the church and its programs will continue, including worship and programs for children and youth. Allow ample time for questions they may have about the transition.

Acknowledge their feelings, using their own language to help them process the experience. Do not use language that negates their feelings, like "Don't be sad," or, "Let's just don't think about that."

When you answer their questions, do so in an age-appropriate manner. Limit explanations of conflict or boundary violations to those that children can understand. They are likely overhearing things that you may need to explain more fully. Do so in a way that respects all those involved and emphasizes that we all fall short of how we would like to behave at times. Reassure them that God is with all of us, even when we make mistakes or behave in ways that are less than kind. Explain without labeling any group or person negatively, using such language as, "People often disagree on very important things because they value them so much," or, "We all make choices sometimes that are not the best, and sometimes there are consequences for those choices," and "No matter what, we continue to love each other, even in times of disagreement or bad choices."

Listen to children and youth about what they would like to see in a new leader if you are searching for a new pastor. Let their answers be as silly or serious as needed. After all, we all hope for leaders that can embrace both the silly and the serious as they lead us in the church. The wisdom of children can also give us insights in our search process we may not otherwise find.

Beyond those basic good practices of handling change with children and youth, additional tools can help them make spiritual meaning out of the changes they are experiencing. Powerful exercises for building on change in spiritual education include:

- Use stories of change in the Bible as a jumping off point for talking about change. The stories of Joseph's life, or the stories of Mary facing her unexpected role in God's story, can be helpful in understanding where God is in times of change.
- Share prayer practices that go beyond simply talking to God. Embodied prayer, such as walking prayers or movement prayers, or even labyrinth walking, can be a way of praying during changes that take away our words for what is happening to us.
- Discuss the way creation illustrates the power of change. Examples might include a river changing course, a caterpillar turning to a butterfly, or the evolution of a plant or animal species over time. God is in these natural wonders even as they change. Have the students share their favorite story of change from the natural world.
- Use the Gospels to discuss how Jesus' ministry changed over time. What did he do differently as he spent longer in ministry? Did Jesus change his mind? (The story of the Syrop-Phoenician woman can be helpful here.) How can we learn from Jesus' example of listening to God about when change is needed in our lives?

Finally, the most transformative experiences are often those where ample opportunities are provided for reflection and peer support. Try the following:

1. Ask children and youth what changes they have experienced/are experiencing in their lives. Have them explain what has helped them cope with change in the past so that they can learn from each other's experiences.
2. Have each child or youth write a letter to God about a change they are struggling with. Use a few Psalms as examples of how the Psalmists both praised God and expressed their anger and questions to God. If they are comfortable, have them share their letters with one another. Close by praying for each other's struggles and celebrations around their change.
3. Work with your church's older youth to develop helpful resources for younger children and youth who will soon go through what they have experienced on the journey from childhood to young adulthood. What lessons would they share? Invite them to interview adults and elders in the congregation to discover the lessons they would share? Then help them package this resource into a form that can be shared with classes that come after them in the life of the church.

With the addition of these thoughtful tools and practices in your church, children and youth can be supported and enriched in their spiritual path during times of transition.

Reflection Questions:

• How does your church approach congregational changes with children and youth?
• What changes might your congregation's children and youth be dealing with in their own lives?

- What activities would you like to try to facilitate learning from change for your younger members?

| 11 |

Cultivating Change Readiness: Being Ready for Change in "Ordinary Time"

As we have explored in previous chapters, change is inevitable for churches. This means that change readiness is crucial for any congregation and its members. The work of cultivating change readiness is worthwhile, even as a million other things fill our to-do lists. If you pause some of that frenetic activity and pause to make your church's soil ready for whatever changes may come, you will be that much less likely to be derailed on the day they arrive. Making the effort to build these structures and processes into the life of the congregation will pay off in so many ways. When we cultivate change readiness:

We learn to embrace the big changes ahead. It turns out that radical change is easier to accept than incremental change. People who are asked to make minor changes in their diet and exercise soon slip back into old habits, even if they have already had a heart attack and been told these changes are essential to their survival. People who are asked and supported in changing their entire lifestyle after a heart attack have a high success rate, compared to those who tried minor changes who were only half as successful at avoiding future cardiac events.[39]

We remember that God calls us to be willing to leave old roads behind, even family, even friends, even community, to follow Jesus down new roads ahead. In fact, the story of Jesus is the story of a community who thought things would go one way, toward a future as a community following a beloved rabbi around, hearing his teachings and loving their neighbors under his guidance – only to find their leader killed by political forces and forced to make a new way without him.

We let go of control. We often seek out the things we can control when faced with unexpected change, which is healthy, to a point. Unfortunately, we can hold on to control so tightly, seeking to preserve and protect what we have left, that we forget that we are called by God to use all our gifts and talents for love and justice.

Knowing and doing all this does not make it easy when life events or a call from God sets us off down a completely different road. However, it can help us travel that hard road. The really good news is that, in congregations, we are not alone on our hard journeys through change.

Building Change Readiness in the Congregation

Advent is my favorite season of the church year. The themes of waiting and readiness do something in my heart. After 11 months of go-go-go, I find I need at least a month of wait to reset things. There is value in Advent waiting, beyond just its interruption of the frantic pace of modern life. However, Advent should not be the only time we consider the value of waiting and readiness in our lives as Christians. Readiness is a frequent theme in Jesus' teachings to his disciples. In the Gospel of Matthew, we find Jesus sharing parables about being ready.

> *"But about that day and hour no one knows, neither the angels of heaven, nor the Son, but only the Father. For as the days of Noah were, so will be the coming of the Son of Man. For as in those days before the*

flood they were eating and drinking, marrying and giving in marriage, until the day Noah entered the ark, and they knew nothing until the flood came and swept them all away, so too will be the coming of the Son of Man. Then two will be in the field; one will be taken and one will be left. Two women will be grinding meal together; one will be taken and one will be left. Keep awake therefore, for you do not know on what day your Lord is coming. But understand this: if the owner of the house had known in what part of the night the thief was coming, he would have stayed awake and would not have let his house be broken into. Therefore you also must be ready, for the Son of Man is coming at an unexpected hour."[40]

Echoing the stories of the Hebrew Bible, when God's people were often surprised by the intervening hand of God, Jesus tells the disciples to be ready, even as they go about their normal daily activities. We cannot know when we will experience the inbreaking of God's presence in our lives, so we must remain ready and watchful, even as we go about our daily activities.

But what does that mean for us today and our churches? As Christians, we are called to set our hearts and minds in such a way as to be receptive to the inbreaking spirit of God. This can be one of the biggest challenges of our faith. Loving our neighbor is no picnic but being open to changing our preferences and routines is a whole other ball game. We all have opportunities to be transformed by the changes that come into our lives. Yet many of us, and many of the organizations we are a part of, remain stubbornly static, unchanged, and even raging against the change that comes to our doors. According to Musselwhite and Plouffe, organizations that are successful in managing change and leveraging it for transformation "no longer view change as a discrete event to be managed, but as a constant opportunity to evolve."[41]

Perhaps the most apt metaphor for readiness is that of hospitality. When you know someone may be coming over to visit, how do you prepare? Do you straighten up the house, make some tea or lemonade, even prepare a few snacks? If you expect them overnight, do you put fresh sheets on the guest bed and give that room some extra attention? Maybe lay out a few towels for them or a robe? Getting ready for guests in our home is somewhat instinctual. We know what to do and just get to it when the time is right. And while most of us are not preparing for guests unless we know they are coming, some people are such masters of hospitality that their homes are always ready for whatever guest their lives may produce. This mastery is the kind of readiness we can aim for in making ourselves and our churches ready for change.

Getting ready for change can be just as instinctual if we are practiced at it. The key is knowing what actions and elements make us ready. Just as fresh sheets and a pot of tea help welcome guests, there are certain characteristics and ways of being that help us welcome change whenever it comes our way.

Experts in organizational development typically measure change readiness by looking at whether an organization has the resources and skills available to navigate change, and enough cooperation and support from members to navigate change, and the capacity to devote enough energy to the change. Marge Combe suggests three indicators that serve to measure change readiness: Capacity, Commitment, and Culture.[42] We can look at these three indicators in churches as well.

Change Culture is the openness of a congregation to change in general and the ways the beliefs and norms of the congregation create positivity or resistance around change, from the smallest changes to the biggest. Culture also captures the ability of members to identify and name resistance and work past it, rather than seeing resistance as a reason to abandon the needed or inevitable change.

Change Commitment is the willingness of the congregation to adapt and change as needed to bring their mission into reality in a changing world. While every member of the congregation does not have to be the biggest cheerleader of change, a few champions or cheerleaders are needed in any successful change effort. For the rest of the members, the quality we are looking for here is *resolve*: the resolve to stick with it and see things through, even when challenging situations arise.

Change Capacity encompasses energy and time. A congregation that is spread too thin or exhausted from too few people doing too much work will likely have greater difficulty with change.

These elements of readiness do not just happen spontaneously. We must create a change-ready system in our church. This is the way that we ensure that when change comes, our congregation is ready. To build change into our congregational system, we need to cultivate the values of change readiness intentionally and openly. Combe also identifies several values that underlie the culture of organizations that stay ready for change, which I have adapted and expanded upon for congregations.[43]

Trust: A healthy congregation is made up of members that trust one another and those they have called as pastors and leaders. Without trust, change efforts are viewed with suspicion and often doomed to fail. Rev. Cameron Trimble, CEO of Convergence, adapts the phrase by Stephen Covey, "Transformation happens at the speed of trust."[44]

Respect: When church members respect one another, change efforts do not succumb to backbiting and other toxic ways of working through conflict. Respecting that everyone in the congregation is doing their best to follow God is essential to changing together.

Transparency: Churches that successfully navigate change model transparency at all levels. Leaders and team update the congregation frequently and fully as to their work. Members are comfortable asking questions about the process at any time.

Accountability: Members of change-ready churches are accountable to one another, both for the work they are doing together and for their ways of relating to one another. If someone fails to uphold the promises they have made or fails to act in trusting, respectful ways, their leaders or peers will call them out on it, respectfully of course, and call them back into a healthy relationship.

Collaboration: Congregations that embrace change also embrace collaboration. To get from point A to point B it will take all hands on deck, as well as lots of perspectives and strategies. Plus, top-down commands to change are rarely effective or lasting. Working together as highly functioning teams is the only way to get there.

Shared Mission: A church that is on a mission is willing to change to make that mission happen. Having a firm sense of a shared mission that permeates every program of the church makes the question "Why do we need to change?" redundant. We change to make our mission a reality.

You may be saying **that all sounds wonderful, but how do we get there from here?**

There are a few key areas you can work on right now to begin getting ready for change. Within any congregational culture are structures and systems that impact the culture around change. You can start here. How do your congregation's ways of working together actually work against change readiness? Combe singles out a few elements of any organizational system that are crucial to change readiness – structures/policies and rewards/penalties. When thinking about your congregation, you need to consider how your structures, policies, rewards, and penalties cultivate change or stop it in its tracks.

Policies: Are your policies barriers to change? Does it take 7 layers of bureaucracy to change the color of the ink on the bulletins? If so, your policies need to change. This may not be step one in building change readiness, as resistance to change will inevitably sideline any changes in bylaws or procedures before they get off the ground. But to be a truly change-ready congregation, your policies and procedures must be agile enough to respond to changing needs and contexts and even brilliant new ideas before they develop cobwebs or die of old age.

Rewards and Penalties: How does your church treat people with new ideas? Or leaders who try something different? If the reaction of even a few members is negative or involves toxic behavior, those people who are skilled in innovation and change will leave your congregation before they are sorely needed in times of transition and adaptation. And if your existing members know that if they step out in a new direction, they will receive nothing but flack, how likely is it that they will try that again soon?

Another place to start is making sure that change readiness is built into every element of your lives together. Aubrey Malphurs points out that change readiness is like muscle memory, in that only changing things up can make a muscle stronger.[45] You must build change into the life of your congregation to avoid atrophy and keep your change muscles strong. One way to do this is to look at the four primary activities of any congregation:

Preaching/Worship: The church's mission and embracing the changes it will bring should be a part of the good news that is proclaimed in your congregation. If it is not the main idea of the sermon, the message should at least acknowledge that the body has a common work and speak to how the themes of the sermon are relevant to that work. Other elements of worship can also provide opportunities to celebrate and proclaim your church's mission and openness to going wherever needed to make it a reality. Prayers can be an opportunity to confess our resistance to change and ask God for help. Song choices can point always to God's capacity for doing new things in our lives if we are open to it. You get the picture. Think strategically about how every element of worship is helping your congregation get ready for change.

Teaching: Teaching healthy conflict skills, healthy ways of relating, and the value of collaboration can go a long way toward readying your church for change. Very few churches have any collective education on these elements of working together well. Education can also expound upon and highlight the necessity of change for your shared mission. Education that does not touch on one of these two areas might be less of a priority until this territory is well covered, such that everyone in the congregation is on the same page about how to work together and what their common work is about. Make time in worship to bless all this as well.

Fellowship: Times of fellowship are perfect opportunities to celebrate your mission and any changes occurring to get there. Have a party! Bless or pray over those doing the work. Also bless and pray over any new initiatives or ways of doing things.

Communication: Be sure to create some common messaging around your common mission. Send out postcards. Create a new tagline for your bulletin or email. Make banners! When you do start a new thing, be sure to celebrate it. Send out announcement cards: Born 2/20/2022, weighing thousands of pounds, our healthy new system of governance/worship service/mission activity! If this is not your congregation's strong suit, invest in a church communications consultant to help you get off on the right foot and then take it from there.[46]

Finally, we can do a few things to increase capacity for change in our system. The cultural pieces above increase psychological capacity. But we must also attend to time and energy as important aspects of our capacity for change. Three key shifts in time and energy can make a huge impact on our change readiness.

Ending exhaustion: Our churches are often spread too thin to even consider any changes. Think of the way any working person is when doing the work of two people due to vacancy or cutbacks. The mere idea of a new software system or form to complete, in order to do their work, feels overwhelming. Our church members can be the same when they are exhausted. The only remedy for this is to cut back all church activities to those which are on task for your church's mission. If that is still too many, keep only the most effective one or two activities. Once people are less exhausted, they will be better able to consider and embrace change.

Creating space: Be sure that all the time your members are at church is not "active time." Make space in your worship and activities for pauses, meditation, prayer. Preach and teach on the importance of these pauses and the importance of Sabbath. Our best energy and ideas often come from a place of centeredness within us, one that is difficult to find if we are constantly in motion.

Making room for spirit: Focus on the role of spirit in all your work together. Too often, church activities, even those helping others, can become mechanical and rote. Take time for reflection after each activity, and during worship, on where God can be seen, and how to listen. This makes room for people to hear how God might be calling them or the congregation to change.

A brief assessment of your congregation's change readiness can be found in the Appendix. It may also be helpful to have your church members do an assessment individually to see where they fall on the scale of change readiness. We offer one at Convergence as part of our comprehensive Vital Church Assessment. Another widely used example is from an older book by Robert Kriegel and David Brandt.[47] I encourage you to take a good look at your congregation and members and identify what muscles you need to build to stay open to change whenever and wherever it occurs. God may be speaking through just those changes.

When we build a change-ready culture in our congregations, a funny thing happens. We often find that our congregation is healthier every day, not only in times of change. Congregations that are not exhausted, that have time and space to listen to God, that communicate in healthy ways, that trust and respect each other, and that have a shared mission are congregations that survive and thrive. We are not only ready for a visit from change when we know it is coming, but any time change comes our way.

We have become Change-Ready Churches that form Change-Ready Christians. The world will be better for it.

| 12 |

Onward into the Change

Simply put, the only constant in life is change. Churches are no place to go to try to hide from change. The world around every church is constantly changing. Each new generation of people brings new characteristics into the church and into the communities churches seek to serve.

Much has been written about the increasing decline in size and number of Christian congregations in the Western world. Congregations that cannot change and adapt will die. Christians who cannot change and learn will be unable to carry the faith into the future. Christians who are ready to face change and transition with open minds and tools for learning, however, will lay the foundation for Christianity to survive and thrive in the coming years, decades, and beyond.

Your congregation can be a part of building that future!

The tools provided in this book and the Appendix are designed to help your church begin to use these practices as a part of your congregational life. However, I would encourage you to not stop there. Stay creative. Play with mindfulness and ritual. Preach radical acceptance that fuels action. Share your gifts and strengthen your community. That way, if tomorrow is the day that your church faces unexpected change, your congregation will be ready to embrace the change and hear where God speaks in transition time. In short, you will be ready for whatever the future may hold.

APPENDIX

1. Change Assessment
2. Worship Resources
3. Small Group Curriculum
4. Children's Curriculum

CHANGE ASSESSMENT FOR CHURCHES

	True	False
1. My church embraces change.		
2. My church regularly does new things in worship.		
3. The members of my church are willing to change in order to achieve our shared goal.		
4. It is easy for new people to join existing church groups at my church.		
5. My church is more comfortable when things remain the same.		
6. New ideas are always welcome at our church		

7. Our members are always willing to try something new at church		
8. Putting a new idea into action at our church takes a long time.		
9. Our church loves the enthusiasm of people with new ideas		
10. In our church, we pride ourselves on our embrace of and success in constantly changing to improve and adapt.		
11. We frequently talk about change during worship and other activities at our church.		

ASSESSMENT SCORING GUIDE

Scoring Guide:

1. T = 1, F = 0
2. T = 1, F = 0
3. T = 1, F = 0
4. T = 1, F = 0
5. T = 0, F = 1
6. T = 1, F = 0
7. T = 1, F = 0
8. T = 0, F = 1
9. T = 1, F = 0
10. T = 1, F = 0
11. T = 1, F = 0

0 - 3 = Change resistant
Your church is significantly resistant to change. You will need to use intentional formation and support to move your congregation through a period of change without significant conflict and decline.

4 - 7 = Change tolerant
Your church will tolerate moderate levels of change. Big changes may cause conflict and dysfunction among more change resistant members. Intentional formation and support can move your congregation and members from merely "getting through it" to learning and transformation.

8 - 11 = Change champion
Your church is great at change. You love trying new things. Make sure to continue providing formation and support so your members become change champions not only at church but in all areas of their lives.

WORSHIP RESOURCES

This is by no means an exhaustive list of worship resources that can support change. It includes songs, prayers and other resources that have been helpful in or that I would use in my own churches as we grappled with change. These resources range from joyful to solemn, from lively to contemplative, from liturgical to conversational, to honor all those aspects of change that may hold spiritual truths for us. The prayers and practices in the small group and children's curriculum may also be used in your worship services.

Hymns

Behold, behold, I make all things new, *Iona Community*[48]

Breathe on Me, Breath of God, *Hymns, Psalms and Spiritual Songs,* 316[49]

Building A New Way, *Singing the Journey,* 1017[50]

Called as Partners in Christ's Service, *Hymns, Psalms and Spiritual Songs,* 343

Colorful Creator, *The New Century Hymnal,* 30[51]

Come to Tend God's Garden, *The New Century Hymnal,* 586

Creator God, Creating Still, *The New Century Hymnal,* 278

Creator Spirit, Come, We Pray, *The New Century Hymnal,* 268

Deep in the Shadows of the Past, *Hymns, Psalms and Spiritual Songs,* 330

Give to the Winds Thy Fears, *Hymns, Psalms and Spiritual Songs,* 286

Give Up Your Anxious Pains, *The New Century Hymnal*, 404

God, Who Stretched the Spangled Heavens, *Hymns, Psalms and Spiritual Songs*, 268

God, You Spin the Whirling Planets, *Hymns, Psalms and Spiritual Songs*, 285

God is Here! As We Your People Meet, *The New Century Hymnal*, 70

God of Change and Glory, *The New Century Hymnal*, 177

God Our Author and Creator, *The New Century Hymnal*, 530

Grant Us Wisdom to Perceive You, *The New Century Hymnal*, 510

Great God, Your Love Has Called Us Here, *Hymns, Psalms and Spiritual Songs*, 353

Great is Thy Faithfulness, *Hymns, Psalms and Spiritual Songs*, 276

Guide My Feet, *Hymns, Psalms and Spiritual Songs*, 354

If Thou but Trust in God to Guide Thee, *Hymns, Psalms and Spiritual Songs*, 282

In the Bulb There is a Flower, *The New Century Hymnal*, 433

In the Midst of New Dimensions, *The New Century Hymnal*, 391

Let Hope and Sorrow Now Unite, *Singing the Living Tradition*, 412[52]

Let us Hope when Hope Seems Hopeless, *The New Century Hymnal*, 278

Like a Tree beside the Waters, *The New Century Hymnal*, 313

Live iInto Hope, *Hymns, Psalms and Spiritual Songs*, 332

My Shepherd Will Supply My Need, *Hymns, Psalms and Spiritual Songs*, 172

Now the Green Blade Rises, *The New Century Hymnal*, 238

O Life that Maketh All Things New, *Singing the Living Tradition*, 12

Open My Eyes That I May See, *Hymns, Psalms and Spiritual Songs*, 324

Renew Your Church, *The New Century Hymnal*, 311

Savior, Like a Shepherd Lead Us, *Hymns, Psalms and Spiritual Songs*, 387

Sheltered by God's Loving Spirit, *The New Century Hymnal*, 368

Sois la Semilla (You Are tThe Seed), *The New Century Hymnal*, 528

Sometimes a Light Surprises, *Glory to God*, 800[53]

Spirit, *Hymns, Psalms and Spiritual Songs*, 319

Spirit of Life, *Singing the Living Tradition*, 123

Standing at the Future's Threshold, *The New Century Hymnal*, 538

The Church of Christ in Every Age, *Hymns, Psalms and Spiritual Songs*, 421

The Wind of Change Forever Blown, *Singing the Living Tradition*, 183

This is a Day of New Beginnings, *The New Century Hymnal*, 417

We Begin Again iIn Love, *Singing the Journey*, 1037

We Gather Here to Bid Farewell, *Hymns, Psalms and Spiritual Songs*, 444

We Limit Not the Truth of God, *The New Century Hymnal*, 316

We Walk by Faith and Not by Sight, *Hymns, Psalms and Spiritual Songs*, 399

When Peace, Like a River (It is Well with My Soul), *The New Century Hymnal*, 438

You Walk along Our Shoreline, *The New Century Hymnal*, 504

Bible stories about change

Abraham's Journey in Genesis 12

Changing Abraham and Sarah's Names in Genesis 17

Paul's Story in Acts 9 and Testimony in Acts 26

Ruth's Experiences in the Book of Ruth

Prayers, Devotionals, and Responsive Readings

Do Not Be Afraid, by Andrew Millard[54]

Change Alone is Unchanging, *Singing the Living Tradition*, 655

Litany for Becoming, by enfleshed[55]

Liturgy for a New Year: A Service of Holy Communion, by Rev. Christine Battjes[56]

O Spirit of Life and Renewal, *Singing the Living Tradition*, 510

Prayer Before Worship, *The New Century Hymnal*, 816

Renewal of Mission, *The New Century Hymnal*, 857

Resurrection, by Paul R. Beedle[57]

Serenity, *The New Century Hymnal*, 852

Struggle and Blessing, service prayers by Rev. Kaji S. Dousa adapted by Susan A. Blain[58]

The Changing and the Fixed, by Leslie Ahuvah Fails[59]

Together, We Arrive[60]

Waiting for Now, by Mandie McGlynn[61]

When I change, by Ma Theresa "Tet" Gustilo Gallardo[62]

Witness to Wonders, service prayers by Rev. Madison Shockley[63]

Spiritual Practices for Times of Transition

Centering Prayer: Change. Anxiety. Fear . . .... Freedom. Healing. Wholeness, by Rev. Deedra Rich[64]

Essential Practices, The Presbyterian Church (U.S.A.)[65]

Prayer Litanies, Center for Contemplative Living[66]

Spiritual Practice and Prayer, Unitarian Universalist Association[67]

We Make the Road by Walking, by Brian McLaren[68]

What is Contemplation, by Richard Rohr/The Center for Action and Contemplation[69]

Full bibliographic details on resources cited can be found in the Endnotes.

CHURCH AFTER: CURRICULUM FOR SMALL GROUPS

Organizing Groups

When organizing small groups, several approaches can be effective. You may choose to start new small groups for this purpose and have a sign-up sheet online. You may choose to ask existing groups to use this curriculum for six weeks. You may also choose to hold whole church events for six weeks and then after a meal, break the groups into tables to cover the material. Or a blend of these approaches might be necessary for your church. Regardless of your approach to forming the groups, it is crucial that the groups have ample time to cover the material, include approximately the same members over time, and are led by trained group leaders.

Timing: Group sessions will take approximately an hour and a half to cover the material. I recommend scheduling 2-hour sessions, with 15 minutes for gathering and refreshments at the beginning and an extra 15 minutes you can use if needed, depending on how quickly you move through the material. Weeknights or Sundays after worship are often best, but if your group is willing to show up earlier than normal for Sunday School, Sunday morning sessions can work.

Group members: If possible, it is ideal to have no more than 12 members per group. While group members can switch groups if needed due to a scheduling issue, it is best to have groups stay together for the entire series. This helps build the relationships needed for support during times of change.

Group Leaders: Choose group leaders that are good at presenting and leading with a non-anxious presence. Those who are the life of the party may not be the best at leading a group, so you may want to consider those stalwart but quieter members, especially those with teaching experience. Invite group leaders personally, do not rely on a blanket call for volunteers. Try to find group leaders whose schedules allow for a variety of times for your small groups. To train your small group leaders, set aside a Saturday to introduce the material and walk them through it together as a small group. This will take most of a day, so make sure to have snacks and lunch provided. While you may be able to skip some of the icebreakers and opening prayers, the substantial material of the course should be done as a group by the leaders-in-training. They should all have experience with all the sessions before leading a group on their own.

Supplies: Group leaders should be provided with (or obtain themselves) pens, paper, a flip chart, a basket of assorted beads, and a basket of lengths of string, yarn, and assorted natural materials (leaves, flowers, branches, rocks, etc.) for the making of a mandala. Group leaders will also need a phone to play the gathering music for each session from YouTube or another music platform. Chairs should be arranged in a circle with the group leader as simply another person in the circle. There should be a small table or other object in the center of the circle for lighting candles and creating the mandala.

SESSION 1: INTRO/SAFE SPACE

Gathering music: Changes, by David Bowie

Welcoming words: As you enter, take a bead that makes you feel at home. Take it to your seat with you and keep it near you during this session.

Opening Prayer:

Silence . . . . . .then

God of change and new life, may the words of our mouths and the meditations of our hearts make your love known in this space, this day, and throughout our lives. Amen.

Scripture: Psalm 102:25-27

Icebreaker:

Tell your name and in one sentence, describe a gift you have received from a time when something in your life changed.

Safe Space Guidelines:

Hand out, each person read one line.

- We are all God's children – known and loved exactly as we are in this very moment. Remember that about each other. Remember that about YOU!
- Avoid interrupting others. Respect fellow group members by honoring the principle that only one person will speak at a time. Try waiting 5 seconds before responding to make sure the previous speaker is finished.

- Be respectful of each other's feelings, and be respectful of all cultures, races, sexual orientations, gender identities, religions, class backgrounds, abilities, and perspectives.
- This group is about honoring each other's insights to discern together. It is not your job to debunk or challenge others' understandings and the language they use to describe them.
- Speak in "I" statements: Do not tell others what to do or think as if it is a command. Instead, describe your own experience.
- Agree not to repeat personal things people say during a group meeting to others.
- "Step up and step back:" If you usually do not talk much, challenge yourself to speak more. If you find yourself talking more than others, challenge yourself to speak less.
- Self-care and group care. Be aware that spiritual topics can be challenging and emotional for group members. As a group, do not judge anyone who becomes emotional or needs to step out either for a few minutes or for the remainder of the meeting.

Closing question:

In one or two sentences, what change is most present in your life right now?

Homework Assignment:

Instruct group members to create a three-minute Testimony of a time they found God or good news in a change in their life. Hand out Instructions.

Close with Prayer:

Ask if anyone would like to pray, if not -

God of the new covenant, as we struggle with change, challenge, and renewal, we remember your ever-presence, and that the story of Jesus and Christianity is a story of changing from old ways to new ways, old rhythms to new ones, and old life to new. May that story come to life in us through our time together.

SESSION 2: TESTIMONY

Gathering Music:

"A Change is Gonna Come" by Sam Cooke

Welcoming Words:

Find a bead that feels like it tells your story. Take it to your seat and keep it with you during our discussions.

Opening Prayer:

Silence . . . . . .then -

God of life-changing days, may the words of our mouths and the meditations of our hearts make your love known in this space, this day, and throughout our lives. Amen.

Scripture: Hebrews 11:8 (Invite a group member to read)

Icebreaker:

In one phrase, name the gift you most hope to receive from participating in this class?

Discussion:

Have participants share a testimony of a time their faith was strengthened in groups of three. Reconvene and facilitate discussion of the following questions:

What was that like for you to share your testimony?

What was that like to hear the testimonies of others?

Homework Assignment:

Instruct group members to create a eulogy for whatever they are leaving behind in a change they are dealing with right now, saying, "Celebrate it as you tell of its life, the gifts it gave to others, what you will most miss, remember and treasure about it, and the wonderful legacy it will leave behind."

Closing question:

In one phrase, describe what your story bead says about you.

Close with Prayer:

Ask if anyone would like to pray, if not -

God of change, you call forth new life and new possibility and for that we give you thanks. All that is before us is yours. Loosen our grip on the things we once were and open our hearts, minds, and hands to the new thing to which you are calling us. You are the God of new beginnings. May it be so. Amen.

SESSION 3: GRIEF AND LOSS

Gathering Music: "Change" by Tracy Chapman

Opening Prayer:

Silence . . . . . .then -

God of our grief and of our sorrows, may the words of our mouths and the meditations of our hearts make your love known in this space, this day, and throughout our lives. Amen.

Scripture: Psalm 23 (Invite a group member to read)

Discussion:

Invite members to read their Eulogies out loud one at a time. If your group is larger than 12, break members into groups of 4 to read their Eulogies.

Invite all members to walk up and place their Eulogies on the table as they take a bead to represent that even when leaving things behind, some things stay with us.

Facilitate discussion on the following questions:

What was that like for you? Writing them? Hearing them?

What was the hardest thing?

How did you feel afterward?

What did you notice in the things others chose to memorialize?

Homework Assignment:

Make an inventory of all the things you might need to let go of during this time of change. Observe how it feels to name those things on your list.

Close with Prayer:

Ask if anyone would like to pray, if not-

God who makes a way in the wilderness. You have named us and claimed us for your own. Abide with us as we move forward. Quench our deepest thirst for the journey before us. Help us to perceive the new thing to be born in our community. When change feels like too big a task to manage, remind us that only when we loosen our grip, will our hands be free to do the work to which you are calling us. Unbind us from the past that we may be a new creation. Amen.

SESSION 4: HOPES AND FEARS

Gathering Music: "Under Pressure" by Queen

Welcoming words:

Pick out a bead to represent your hope for this change, and a bead to represent your fear about what the change will mean/bring. Take these to hold during our discussion.

Opening Prayer:

Silence . . . . . .then -

God of our hopes and of our fears, may the words of our mouths and the meditations of our hearts make your love known in this space, this day, and throughout our lives. Amen.

Scripture: Matthew 6:25-34 (Invite a group member to read)

Discussion:

How did it feel to name things you might have to let go of during this change?

What are you most fearful about for this change in your life?

What hopes do you have for this change in your life?

Final Activity:

Using large paper, invite the group to each write one thing they are willing to let go of to make room for God's new things. Debrief by having each person read their entry aloud, followed by the group response, *Thank you, Lord, for this loving gift.*

Homework Assignment:

Ask group members to pair up with the person they know the least about in the group and ask them these questions: What is your greatest gift or talent? What are you most passionate about? What is your biggest dream for the future?

Close with Prayer:

Ask if anyone would like to pray, if not -

Comforting God, we know even in our fears and in our hopes, you are with us. You surround us with your love, that we might surround each other with love, keeping worry at bay, lessening fear, and building up hope. Help us remember that, and share that love with all we encounter. Amen.

SESSION 5: GIFTS AND PASSIONS

Music: "If You Want to Sing Out" by Cat Stevens

Icebreaker:

What do you need in your suitcase for your journey through change?

Opening Prayer

Silence . . . . . .then -

God of gifts and of passions, may the words of our mouths and the meditations of our hearts make your love known in this space, this day, and throughout our lives. Amen.

Scripture: Romans 12:6-8

Discussion:

Lead the group in debriefing their interviews. Have each person introduce the person they interviewed. What was the most interesting gift, passion, dream that they heard in the interview?

Invite each participant to give one bead to their interview partner.

Closing: Give the following instructions for sharing - In one sentence, name the gift you are most excited about using during and after the change you are experiencing.

Homework Assignment:

Begin to envision how you might use your gifts and passions to help you navigate the change ahead. What prior experiences have prepared you for such a time as this? How might you also ask for assistance from those in this room or your world with different gifts and passions than your own? How can they be way finders for you in this change? Journal your thoughts, by simply writing them out, putting them in creative form as a prayer or poem, or drawing a picture to express them.

Close with Prayer:

Ask if anyone would like to pray, if not -

God of all our gifts, help us to use them above all to be as you would have us be, to do as you would have us do, and to love as you would have us love. Amen.

SESSION 6: THE ROAD AHEAD

Gathering Music: "Feeling Good" by Nina Simone

Icebreaker:

What do you most need from this community to help you on your journey of change?

Opening Prayer:

Silence . . . . . .then -

God of journeys and of destinations, may the words of our mouths and the meditations of our hearts make your love known in this space, this day, and throughout our lives. Amen.

Scripture: 1 Thessalonians 5

Discussion:

Facilitate discussion on the questions -

What do you envision for yourself on the road ahead?

What do you think you are learning on your journey of change?

Music and Mandala:

Put on a selection of meditative instrumental music and give the following instructions -

Today, community, we are going to create a mandala. Mandala is a Sanskrit word for circle. In the circle, we find compassion, safety, wholeness, and grace. During the music, I invite you to come and help create a Mandala. The mandala that we create as a community will exist only in this time and space. After the service, it will be dismantled, reminding us that all times in life are transitions and part of the larger journey. We do not hold onto past moments but look forward to creating more as we live within our individual callings. While we build the Mandala, take as many beads as you like, feel free to use some in the Mandala, maybe grab one more bead to remember our journey together, feel free to grab some string if you would like to keep one or more of your beads as a companion on your journey.

Close with Prayer:

Beloved ones – You have a journey ahead. May God himself, the God who makes everything holy and whole, make you holy and whole, put you together – spirit, soul, and body – and keep you fit for all that you encounter in the days to come. Amen.

SEE, I AM DOING A NEW THING: A CHILDREN'S CURRICULUM

Children deal with change all the time, possibly more than us as adults. This curriculum is designed to help children explore the theme of change in the frame of our Christian faith. Lessons provide opportunity for learning a Bible verse, for sharing stories with each other, for discussion with and among the children, and for a creative time illustrating themes of the lesson. Each of these six lessons is short enough to be offered during a Sunday morning education time or if children leave the sanctuary during a portion of worship. These lessons align somewhat with the adult small group curriculum.

Session 1

Opening Prayer: God of change and new life, be with us in this space, this day, and throughout our lives. Amen.

Scripture: Psalm 102: 25-27 (Easy to Read Version[70] recommended)

Opening: Tell your name and an animal whose name starts with the same letter of your name.

Children respond.

Teacher read: We are all God's children—known and loved exactly as we are in this very moment. Remember that about each other. Remember that about YOU!

Teacher read: What is a big change that you can remember happened to you?

Children respond.

Teacher read: What did it feel like when things changed in a big way?

Children respond.

Teacher read: The story of Jesus is a story of changing from old ways to new ways, old rhythms to new ones, and old life to new. Every week this season we will talk about change and how it happens in our lives, and how we can find God in those changes. Today we will start by using the art supplies on the table to create a picture of a time change was a good thing in your life.

Children do art projects.

Teacher read: Let's take turns sharing our pictures and telling what is in them.

Children share.

Teacher read: Will you pray with me? God, we thank you for being with us when changes are a good thing, and when changes are hard. Amen.

SESSION 2

Opening Prayer: God of life-changing days, make your love known in this space, this day, and throughout our lives. Amen.

Scripture: Hebrews 11:8 (International Children's Bible[71] recommended)

Opening: What is your name and what is the best gift you have ever received?

Children share.

Teacher read: What did it feel like to get such a special gift?

Children share.

Teacher read: God gives us gifts in many ways. Today we will use the art supplies on the table to create a picture of a gift you think of when you think of God.

Children do art projects.

Teacher read: Did you ever have to change anything to make room for a new gift? Move things around or give something away?

Children share.

Teacher read: What was it like having to give something up to get something new?

Children share.

Teacher read: What was it like having to give something up to get something new?

Children share.

Teacher read: Will you pray with me? God of change, your love gives generously. All the gifts in our lives show us your love. For that we give you thanks. Amen.

SESSION 3

Opening Prayer: God of our grief and of our sorrows, make your love known in this space, this day, and throughout our lives. Amen

Scripture: Psalm 23 (International Children's Bible recommended)

Opening: Say your name and say something that you have ever lost.

Children share.

Teacher read: Have you ever lost something or someone and it made you sad? What was it?

Children share.

Teacher read: What did you love about the thing you lost?

Children share.

Teacher read: When we lose something we love very much, sometimes we make a memorial, or a way to remember what we lost, using words, pictures, or other ways of being creative. Use the art supplies on the table to create a memorial for something you loved that you have lost.

Children do art projects.

Teacher read: Now I would like us to go around and share our art, and tell each other about the things we made a memorial about.

Children share.

Teacher read: When things change, sometimes we are sad. Making sure to remember what we have lost can help us feel God's comfort when we are sad.

Teacher read: Will you pray with me? God of comfort and love, we know you are with us when we are sad. Thank you for helping us remember the people and things that are no longer with us. Amen.

SESSION 4

Opening Prayer: God of our hopes and of our fears, make your love known in this space, this day, and throughout our lives. Amen

Scripture: Matthew 6:25-34 (International Children's Bible recommended)

Opening: Say your name and say something that makes you feel scared.

Children share.

Teacher read: When things change, sometimes it can be scary. Have you ever been scared about a big change in your life? What was that like?

Children share.

Teacher read: What helps you when you feel scared?

Children share.

Teacher read: When we feel scared, all the things that make us feel better are gifts from God. Use the art supplies on the table to make a picture of something that makes you feel scared on one side of the paper, and something that makes you feel better on the other side.

Children do art projects.

Teacher read: Now I would like us to go around and share our art, and tell each other about the things that make us feel scared and the things that make us feel better.

Children share.

Teacher read: When things change, sometimes we are scared. God is with us, though, and all the things that make us feel better are gifts from God.

Teacher read: Will you pray with me? God of comfort and love, we know you are with us when we are scared. Thank you for helping us face the things that scare us. Amen.

SESSION 5

Opening Prayer: God of all of our gifts and talents, make your love known in this space, this day, and throughout our lives. Amen.

Scripture: Romans 12:6-8 (EasyEnglish 2018 Bible[72] recommended)

Opening: Say your name and say something that you are good at.

Children share.

Teacher read: When things change, sometimes we must pitch in and help. Have any of you helped your family or class with something recently? What did you help with?

Children share.

Teacher read: Did you know we are all different in what we are good at and how we can help? Why do you think we are all good at helping in different ways?

Children share.

Teacher read: When things are changing, we need to use what we are good at to help others. Use the art supplies on the table to make a picture of you doing something you are good at.

Children do art projects.

Teacher read: Now I would like us to go around and share our art, and tell each other about the things that we are good at.

Children share.

Teacher read: Did any of you notice something someone is good at that you are not good at? God made us all good at different things so that together we are a great team. Now that you know what all of you are good at, do not be afraid to ask for help with those things you are not good at. Will you pray with me? God, thank you for making us all good at different things. Amen.

SESSION 6

Opening Prayer: God of going to new places, make your love known in this space, this day, and throughout our lives. Amen

Scripture: 1 Thessalonians 5:14b-18 (International Children's Bible recommended)

Opening: Say your name and say something you like about the person sitting next to you.

Children share.

Teacher read: When things change, sometimes we must encourage each other. Does anyone know what encourage means?

Children share.

Teacher read: Did you know we all need encouragement sometimes? What are some ways we can encourage those around us?

Children share.

Teacher read: Use the art supplies on the table to make a card to encourage someone.

Children do art projects.

Teacher read: Now I would like us to go around and share our art, and tell each other about how our cards could encourage someone.

Children share.

Teacher read: We will definitely have times in our lives and in our church when things will change. We can use the things we learned in this class to remember those things we miss, to face our fears, to use our gifts to help the team, and to encourage each other. Now you can all be change champions. Will you pray with me? God, thank you for bringing us together, giving us gifts and the power of encouragement, and comforting us when things are hard. Thank you for making us better change champions, every day. Amen.

ENDNOTES

[1] 2 Corinthians 5:17-19, New Revised Standard Version (NRSV)

[2] Saladdin Rumi, *Rumi: Selected Poems*, trans. Coleman Barks with John Moynce, A. J. Arberry, Reynold Nicholson (New York: Penguin Books, 2004)

[3] Max Rollwage, Alisa Loosen, Tobias U. Hauser, et al, "Confidence drives a neural confirmation bias," *Nature Communications* 11, 2634 (May 2020). https://doi.org/10.1038/s41467-020-16278-6; Drew Westen, Paul S. Blagov., Keith Harenski, et al., "Neural bases of motivated reasoning: An fMRI study of emotional constraints on partisan political judgment in the 2004 U.S. presidential election," *Journal of Cognitive Neuroscience* 18(11), (November 2006), 1947-1957

[4] Westen, et al., "Neural bases of motivated reasoning."

[5] Mezirow, Jack. "Learning to think like an adult," in *Learning as Transformation: Critical Perspectives on a Theory in Progress*, ed. Mezirow Jack, et al. (San Francisco, CA: Jossey-Bass, 2000), 3-33.

[6] Westen, et al., "Neural bases of motivated reasoning."

[7] Fleischer, B. J. "The ministering community as context for religious education: A case study of St. Gabriel's catholic parish," *Religious Education* 101(1), 104-122. (2006).

[8] Hilary Scarlett, *Neuroscience for Organizational Change: An Evidence-based Practical Guide to Managing Change* (2016).

[9] Bridges, William, *Managing Transitions: Making the Most of Change* (Reading, Mass: Addison-Wesley, 1991).

[10] J. Russell Crabtree, *Transition Apparitions: Why Much of What We Know about Pastoral Transitions Is Wrong* (Self-published: Magi Press, 2015)

[11] Anna Hall, *Informal and incidental learning during congregational leadership transitions,* University of Georgia, 2016), http://getd.libs.uga.edu/pdfs/hall_anna_m_201605_phd.pdf

[12] Karen E. Watkins and Victoria J. Marsick, "Group and organizational learning," Kasworm, Carol E., et al, *Handbook of Adult and Continuing Education* (Thousand Oaks, CA, SAGE, 2010), 59-70; Mary Ziegler, ""Awakening": Developing Learning Capacity in a Small Family Business," *Advances in Developing Human Resources* 1 (1999): 52 - 65.

[13] Barbara J. Fleischer, "The ministering community as context for religious education: A case
study of St. Gabriel's catholic parish," *Religious Education* 101(1) (2006), 104-122.

[14] Raimonda Alonderienė and Asta Pundzienė, "The significance of formal, informal and non-formal learning for the acquisition of the change management competence." *Vocational Education: Research & Reality* 15 (2008), 173-180.

[15] Loren B. Mead, *A Change of Pastors: ...And How It Affects Change in the Congregation* (Bethesda, MD: Alban Institute, 2005).

[16] Kara Witherow, "Centenary UMC's Roving Listeners listen, learn, love," Retrieved from https://www.sgaumc.org/newsdetail/centenary-umc-partners-with-local-group-to-combat-period-poverty-12972816, June 2021.

[17] Molly Phinney Baskette, *Standing naked before God: The art of public confession* (Cleveland: Pilgrim Press, 2015).

[18] Genesis 12, NRSV

[19] Exodus 6-9, NRSV

[20] Brian D. McLaren, *The Great Spiritual Migration: How the World's Largest Religion is Seeking a Better Way to Be Christian* (London: Hodder & Stoughton, 2017).